Julie Stafford

TASTE OF LIFE

VIKING

Viking
Penguin Books Australia Ltd
487 Maroondah Highway, PO Box 257
Ringwood, Victoria 3134, Australia
Penguin Books Ltd
Harmondsworth, Middlesex, England
Penguin Putnam Inc.
375 Hudson Street, New York, New York 10014, USA
Penguin Books Canada Limited
10 Alcorn Avenue, Toronto, Ontario, Canada M4V 3B2
Penguin Books (NZ) Ltd
Cnr Rosedale and Airborne Roads, Albany, Auckland, New Zealand
Penguin Books (South Africa) (Pty) Ltd
4 Pallinghurst Road, Parktown 2193, South Africa

First published by Greenhouse Publications 1983
First published by Penguin Books Australia Ltd 1993
This edition published 1998

10 9 8 7 6 5 4 3 2 1

Cover design by Cathy Larsen, Penguin Design Studio
Text design by Leonie Stott, Penguin Design Studio
Photography by Mark Chew
Food preparation and styling by Fiona Hammond
Illustrations by Michelle Ryan
Typeset by Post Pre-press Group, Brisbane, Queensland
Printed in Australia by Australian Print Group, Maryborough, Victoria

National Library of Australia
Cataloguing-in-Publication data:

Stafford, Julie.
    Taste of life.

Rev. ed.
Includes index.
ISBN 0 670 87578 3.

1. Cookery (Natural foods). I. Title.

641.5637

FRONT COVER
PHOTOGRAPH:
*Vegetable
casserole with
orange swede
sauce (see
page 71).*

Contents

Introduction

In 1983 I nervously held in my hands the very first copy of *Taste of Life*. This cookbook was a record of my kitchen experiments, lovingly carried out in my search to find a simple approach to healthy eating. Three years before my husband Bruce, only 30 years of age, had been diagnosed with Hodgkin's disease (cancer of the lymphatic system). As I watched his body succumb to the devastating effects of traditional invasive treatments, I reasoned that we needed to find a way to help Bruce's body get well again while building a strong immune system to prevent the return of the disease.

It seemed such commonsense to me that while the doctors worked to kill Bruce's cancer cells, I could create a balance by working to nourish the cancer-free cells. I searched extensively for information on the body's essential nourishment needs and the message was always the same – the human body is one of the most magnificent masses of living cells alive today, constantly sloughing off billions of dead cells every day and recreating itself with the production of billions of new cells. Who we are and how healthy we are is very much determined by our genetic structure and the nourishment provided to that structure. For its survival, its function and its ability to perform and endure beyond an average level, this mass of cells needs to be nourished with a good source of protein for growth and repair; complex carbohydrates for energy; vitamins and minerals for vitality and function; essential fats for insulation, organ protection and energy; micro-nutrients for vitamin and mineral absorption; and of course pure water to help carry these nutrients around the body.

My new-found knowledge, knowledge that I had either not learnt at school or well and truly forgotten, gave me a new attitude to food, its purpose, how it might play a role in Bruce's recovery, and just as importantly, how it could benefit my own health. The Taste of Life philosophy – 'What we eat should be good for us and taste good' – was born. Like most people, I hadn't thought too much about the role food played in determining my health. I had eaten food for its taste and visual impact. I often chose foods introduced to me via television or magazine promotions, and I cooked recipes I had seen my mother prepare.

The benefits of our changed diet were immediate. We had to adjust to a different taste, which brought about a new life for us both. Bruce and I experienced a vitality never felt before. I managed to lose weight eating more food than I ever had. Bruce's health returned and he continues to be cancer-free, 18 years after the diagnosis. Most people don't make changes to their eating habits until there is a crisis in the form of an illness or a considerable weight gain. Our growing awareness and our enjoyment of the benefits constantly remind Bruce and I not to take our health for granted.

Who could have imagined the impact this book would have. In the first few weeks of publication, more than 40 000 copies of the book disappeared from the bookshelves. It has gone on to sell a million copies throughout Australia, New Zealand, the United States and the United Kingdom. Obviously I was not the only person who understood the need for such a commonsense, simple approach to eating!

Today, 15 years after the first publication of *Taste of Life*, the message remains the same; in fact it's now probably more relevant. According to the Australian Bureau of Statistics, an alarming 40 per cent of Australians (45 per cent men and 35 per cent women) are overweight or obese, and the figure is rising. Over 350 000 Australians have been diagnosed with diabetes, and it's estimated that over 300 000 more people have the disease, but don't know it. Someone dies every 10 minutes in Australia due to heart disease and every 20 minutes someone dies due to cancer. Recent studies show that 30–35 per cent or 1 in 3 Australian children are too fat, and 50 per cent of 10–15-year-olds have high blood cholesterol levels. It's estimated that 50 per cent of adult Australians have an elevated cholesterol level (over 5.5 mmol/L).

The World Health Organization (WHO) agrees that two-thirds of all disease today is directly linked to diet, lifestyle and stress. To prevent and manage many of these diseases, WHO recommends we follow some basic principles:

- Eat a diet low in fat, especially saturated fat.

- Eat a diet high in fibre, especially from vegetables, fruits, cereals, grains, legumes.

- Eat plenty of fresh fruits and vegetables.

- Eat from a wide variety of nutritious food sources.

- Eat a diet low in added refined sugar.

- Eat a diet low in added salt.

- Limit alcohol intake.

- Avoid smoking.

- Maintain a healthy body weight.

- Avoid processed and smoked foods, and foods with additives and preservatives.

Of course we can still occasionally indulge in the foods to which we have become accustomed beyond the simple Taste of Life philosophy. However if we are serious about achieving good health and avoiding disease, we need to eliminate as many of the health risk factors as possible. We need to remember that the function of food is first and foremost that of survival. Its purpose is to nourish, cleanse, revitalise and regenerate our whole being and in so doing create our life force.

The Taste of Life philosophy has heralded a new awareness of the vital role food plays in developing and maintaining good health. This book is designed to be an effective, simple tool to help you achieve real health results easily – every day. The recipes in this book will help you create a healthy eating regime that suits your own physical needs and offers many different taste options. I hope you, like my family, enjoy a whole new taste of life.

Best wishes and good health!

Acknowledgements

I would very much like to thank my family for their enthusiastic encouragement and support for my journey into writing healthy-eating cookbooks, which has brought us all immeasurable rewards.

I would also like to take this opportunity to thank Sally Milner and Peter Steer with whom I began this journey at Greenhouse Publications. They taught me so much about the art of writing and how, once written, a book is nothing without a successful book promotion tour. My grateful thanks to all at Penguin, especially Bob Sessions and Julie Gibbs, who dared to take on the Taste of Life titles and continue the journey with me. Thankyou to my present editor, Helen Pace, who shapes and moulds my material magnificently, and to those who have done so in the past. Through your guidance, wonderful support and friendship, we have accomplished much together.

Thankyou to all those magazines, newspapers, radio stations and television programs who have shared my Taste of Life books with their readers, listeners and viewers. At first these interviews were somewhat daunting, but I have come to know many of you over the years and I always look forward to the next time we meet.

And of course thankyou to the public, who are avid readers and collectors of the Taste of Life series of cookbooks. Your appetite for easy to follow, everyday recipes for healthy eating amazes me!

The basics
of healthy eating

The key to healthy eating is recognising the importance of a healthy diet and your responsibility for creating your own health and maintaining a healthy weight. Think carefully about the food you're eating and eat a wide variety of fresh vegetables, fruits, rice, legumes (dried peas, lentils, beans), wholegrain cereals, wholegrain breads, fish, lean meats, low-fat dairy products or dairy alternatives, nuts and seeds. Eat your food slowly and chew well.

You should try to avoid or reduce your intake of the following:

♦ Foods that contain saturated fats (butter; margarine; lard; ghee; all cooking fats and oils; copha; coconut oil; fatty meats; poultry skin; full-fat and hard cheeses; full-fat ice-creams; full-fat milk; full-fat flavoured milk drinks; full-fat yoghurt; goat's milk; cream; mayonnaise; packaged biscuits; toasted breakfast cereals including toasted muesli; cakes; pastries; some cereals; some muesli bars; confectionery, especially chocolate; snack foods like chips, some popcorn, Twisties, Cheezels).

♦ Foods that are cooked in fats or cooking oils (home-cooked deep-fried meals; barbeques with a greasy cooking surface; fish and chips; hamburgers; cheeseburgers; fritters; stirfries with oil; fried rice, especially with added bacon and eggs; toasted sandwiches with butter; most takeaway foods).

♦ Processed meats – they are high in fat and sodium.

- Smoked and cured meats – they are high in fat and sodium as well as cancer-causing nitrites.

- Organ meats (brains, liver, kidney, tongue, heart) – they are all high in fat and cholesterol.

- Breads made with added cheese or bacon or garlic butter.

- Specialty breads such as croissants and brioche – they are high in fat.

- Pastas made with rich sauces and added cheese.

- Pizza made with meat and/or seafood and full-fat cheese toppings.

- Seafood like prawns, shrimp, calamari, octopus, caviar, squid. Although low in fat these are all high in cholesterol.

- Egg yolks (large numbers of). The yolk is high in saturated fat and cholesterol. If your cholesterol level is over 5.5 mmol/L you may need to reduce your intake.

- Avocado and olives (large numbers of). Although they contain 'good' fat (monounsaturated fat), they both contain a lot of it.

- High-fat meals like eggs and bacon for breakfast.

- Coffee, alcohol, cola drinks, tea – they dehydrate the body.

- Sugary 'quick-fix' snacks such as muesli bars, chocolate, jelly beans and boiled lollies.

- Nuts (large numbers of), especially the salted varieties. Although they contain 'good' fat (monounsaturated fat), they contain a lot of it.

Did
you know?

- Our body needs at least eight glasses of water a day for good health. Water tastes great, it helps curb an appetite, it has no calories, it removes toxins from the body, and it hydrates and carries nourishment to our cells.

- Our body requires on average approximately 200 mg of sodium daily. Australians, on average, are presently consuming 2300–4500 mg of sodium (via salt). We add too much salt at the table and in the cooking process, but the most sodium is consumed from processed and takeaway foods. Salt can be replaced in the diet by substituting herbs or a squeeze of lemon juice.

- Australians eat on average 15–20 g fibre daily. We need to eat at least 30 g for good health. This amount of fibre can be found in a bowl of high-fibre cereal, three slices of high-fibre bread, two pieces of fresh fruit or vegetables, a small can of beans or half to one cup of pasta or brown rice. Fibre is essential in our diet. It provides bulk as well as a feeling of fullness, which can prevent us from overeating. It helps avoid constipation by speeding up the movement of digested foods through the bowel, and it helps create a healthy digestive system. It also reduces cholesterol.

- There are three types of fat. Saturated fat (the most harmful) is found mostly in animal products and raises blood cholesterol. Monounsaturated fat (found mostly in oils such as olive and canola oils, nuts, seeds and some vegetables like avocado) actually helps lower blood cholesterol if eaten with a meal in which the saturated fat content is low, for example a salad, vegetables or a pasta dish. Polyunsaturated fat, found in vegetable oils, margarines, nuts and seeds, works like monounsaturated fats. All fats are high in calories.

◆ Australians eat 48 kg sugar per person per year (or 25 teaspoons daily). Most of this sugar comes in less obvious forms: in processed foods, cakes, biscuits, confectionery, fizzy drinks, cordials, ice-creams, sauces and cereals. An average can of soft drink contains 10 teaspoons of sugar; a chocolate bar 8 teaspoons; an ice-cream 6 teaspoons; and a sweet biscuit 2 teaspoons. A bowl of cereal (before adding sugar) can be comprised of between 1 per cent and 40 per cent sugar.

◆ Fresh fruits and vegetables (especially citrus fruits containing vitamin C and vegetables like cabbage, broccoli and brussels sprouts) have enzymes that protect against cancer.

◆ Smoked and cured foods contain nitrites, which are directly linked to some forms of cancer.

◆ A cup of instant coffee contains approximately 90 mg caffeine; a cappuccino 105 mg; a cup of strong tea 50 mg; a can of Coca-Cola 50 mg; and a small bar of chocolate 33 mg. Caffeine has been linked to headaches, insomnia, irritability and dehydration.

◆ Potatoes that have gone green or have sprouted can make you sick. The substance that makes potatoes green is a form of poison.

◆ The average adult requires only 90–125 g lean meat per day (all visible fat removed before cooking). The body turns excess protein into fat.

◆ Alcohol can raise triglycerides (a fat that occurs naturally in the blood) and blood pressure as well as add extra calories to your diet.

- You can maximise the nutritional value of vegetables by cooking them with peel or skin on, as most nutrients lie just below the surface. Cut vegetables into large portions and cook slowly with a minimum of water or, preferably, steam vegetables by allowing them to cook in their own moisture. Eat vegetables as soon as they are cooked, as when left to stand for too long vegetables lose valuable nutrients.

- There are two types of cholesterol. 'Bad' cholesterol, Low Density Lipoprotein (LDL), builds up on the inside of blood vessel walls when you eat too much saturated fat. This is a precursor to heart disease and stroke. 'Good' cholesterol, High Density Lipoprotein (HDL), removes the LDL cholesterol from blood vessel walls and takes it to the liver where it's broken down and removed from the body. Omega 3 fatty acid, contained in fish and seafood, helps promote the production of HDL.

- Processed foods contain fewer nutrients and less fibre, and usually have large amounts of added sugar, salt and fat.

- A healthy diet is one that includes at least two servings of fruit and five servings of vegetables daily.

- Toasted cereals are cooked in oil. They have about 20 per cent more calories than untoasted varieties.

- The word 'Light' (or 'Lite') that appears on some food products *does not* mean the product is low in fat. It may mean that it's light in colour or flavour.

- The words 'reduced fat' that appear on some food products *do not* mean the product is low in fat. It may mean that some fat has been cut from the product, but it can still have a high fat content. Check the fat value on the label to be sure.

- Plant foods do not contain cholesterol – only animal products do.

Making the most
of your ingredients

APPLE JUICE CONCENTRATE

Apple juice concentrate is apple juice boiled to make a syrup. It contains vitamins, minerals and water-soluble fibre (pectin), and is used in recipes as a refined sugar substitute. Apple juice concentrate has approximately 30 calories per tablespoon compared with honey, which has 61 calories per tablespoon, and refined sugar, which has 64 calories. When converting recipes, the general rule is to substitute half a cup of apple juice concentrate for every 1 cup of refined sugar. (You may need more or less depending on how sweet you like your food.) Apple juice concentrate can be reconstituted to make apple juice by adding 250 ml water to 1 tablespoon apple juice concentrate. Apple juice concentrate keeps well for a long time in the refrigerator.

BAKING POWDER (sodium-free)

All the recipes in this book requiring flour and baking powder use a commercial baking powder. However, to maintain a diet very low in sodium you can make your own sodium-free baking powder by using equal quantities – say, 2 tablespoons each – of cornflour, cream of tartar and potassium bicarbonate (available from chemists). Sift ingredients together and store in an airtight container. Shake well before using. Use approximately 2 teaspoons to every cup of flour. This baking powder will begin to react once it combines with moisture so you need to work with it quickly and then get the mixture into the oven quickly.

BEVERAGES

Water is the best beverage you can drink. Fresh juices are also good, and are better than bottled juices. If you must buy bottled juices, look for sugar-free, preservative-free varieties. Herbal teas and coffee substitutes are delicious, and fizzy drinks can be made simply by adding mineral water or soda water to fresh fruit juices or fruit concentrates. Look for low-alcohol beers and wines and limit your intake to 1 or 2 glasses per day. Alcoholic drinks have a dehydrating effect on the body, so you should drink more water on the days you drink alcohol.

BISCUITS

Choose low-fat, low-salt biscuits that contain fibre. Look for ingredients such as wholemeal flour, bran, rolled oats or rice. A low-salt biscuit should have a sodium level of less than 120 mg per 100 g serve. There is a wide variety from which to choose, including rice cakes, water crackers, oatmeal crackers, Vita-Weat and Ryvita.

BREAD

Buy bread that is low in fat, low in salt, and which is either high in fibre or contains grains. There is a wide variety of breads from which to choose, including wholemeal, multigrain, rye, kibbled wheat, sourdough, high-fibre white, oat and barley, pita and Lebanese (ideal with fillings or as a pizza base), fruit, and pumpernickel. Soy breads are becoming popular because they contain phytoestrogens which are vital for the prevention of breast cancer and heart disease, but they are high in fat.

BUTTERMILK

Originally buttermilk was the liquid remaining after butter had been separated from milk or cream. Today buttermilk is made by adding selected bacteria to low-fat milk. It's slightly acidic in flavour, and is thicker than milk (but thinner than yoghurt) in consistency. Nutritionally it compares with skim milk with a maximum fat content of around 0.8 per cent. Buttermilk can be substituted for milk in any recipe.

CANNED FISH
Look for varieties in spring water without added salt.

CANNED FRUITS
Look for fruits in natural juice without added sugar. Drain the juice from the fruit before eating.

CANNED TOMATOES
Look for tomatoes in natural juice without added salt.

CAROB
This is a fine dark powder used in cakes, desserts and drinks, usually as a chocolate substitute in a healthy diet. Unlike chocolate, it contains no caffeine or theobromine (often associated with headaches), has fewer calories, contains more protein and also B-group vitamins, calcium, magnesium, potassium and iron.

CEREALS
Breakfast cereals can be loaded with hidden fats, sugar (as much as 40 per cent added sugar) and salt, so it's important to become a label reader. Toasted and crunchy cereals tend to be high in fat. Look for cereals with a fat content below 8 g per 100 g serve (and a fibre content above 10 g per 100 g serve). Some cereals may be low in added sugar but have a high dried fruit content. This might make them a healthier option, but in fact they are still a high-energy food. Look for cereals with a sugar content of less than 20 g per 100 g serve or less than 25 g per 100 g serve if they contain dried fruits. Again, there is a wide variety of breakfast cereals from which to choose, including rolled oats (raw or cooked), sugar-free untoasted muesli, Vita-Brits, Weet-Bix, Weeties, Rice Flakes, Bran

Flakes, Mini Wheats, Shredded Wheats, All Bran, Puffed Wheat, Just Right and Sultana Bran.

CHEESE

Most varieties of hard cheese are high in fat, while the low-fat varieties tend to lack taste and are high in added salt. The best idea is to cut back on the amount of cheese you eat either as a snack, in sandwiches or in the cooking process – it's much better to use a small amount of your favourite sharp-tasting cheese than to use two or three times the amount of a low-fat alternative. Combine grated cheese with breadcrumbs or finely chopped fresh herbs to make it go further. Low-fat hard cheeses (best used in cooking) should have a fat content of less than 10 g per 100 g serve. Other low-fat cheeses include wet cheeses like cottage cheese (contains around 0.4 per cent fat), low-fat ricotta cheese (contains between 1 and 10 per cent fat), low-fat creamed cheese, and low-fat quark. Look for varieties of these cheeses with a fat content of less than 5 g per 100 g serve. Cheese that has a fat content over 5 g per 100 g serve should be used only in moderation. *See also* cottage cheese; ricotta cheese.

COCONUT

Coconut is high in polyunsaturated fats, but you need only a small amount to flavour recipes. (Shredded coconut should be used sparingly.) To make a low-fat coconut-flavoured milk, place 1 cup low-fat milk and 1 tablespoon shredded coconut in a blender and blend until smooth. Allow to stand for at least 2 hours before using in cooking to flavour cakes, desserts, sauces or Thai-style stirfries.

CORNFLOUR

Cornflour is a finely ground powder made from corn, wheat or a combination of both. It's mixed with a liquid (water, stock, milk) to make a paste and used as a thickening agent. Always mix cornflour with a cold liquid. Store in an airtight container in the pantry.

COTTAGE CHEESE

Low-fat cottage cheese is an ideal spread for biscuits and sandwiches, and a great filling for baked potatoes or combined with vegetables in filo pastry triangles. Blend it to a smooth consistency with some low-fat milk and a squeeze of lemon juice to make low-fat sour cream, and substitute it in dessert recipes that call for full-fat cream cheese. *See also* cheese.

DRIED FRUITS

These include apricots, apples, raisins, figs, dates, sultanas, currants, bananas, peaches, nectarines and pears. They make ideal quick energy snacks, but they are high in natural sugar so have only small quantities at a time. When using in cake or dessert recipes, dried fruits can be soaked in water to soften and release some of the fruit sugars.

EGGS

Egg yolks are a nutritious food but are high in saturated fat and cholesterol. Use whole eggs in your diet in moderation; two egg yolks per week in the average diet is enough. Two egg whites will replace one whole egg in most recipes. When folding beaten egg whites into a recipe, always do so using a metal spoon as wooden spoons tend to absorb the air from the egg whites.

EVAPORATED LOW-FAT MILK

This is pure skim milk with 60 per cent water removed. It contains 0.5 per cent fat and no sugar. It has a heavier texture than low-fat milk and is a good substitute in recipes calling for full-fat milk or cream. Chilled evaporated milk whips beautifully to make a light low-fat cream to serve with desserts or as the base of a low-fat ice-cream to which you can add vanilla essence and fruit purées.

FISH/SEAFOOD

Fish contains valuable Omega 3 fatty acid and should be consumed at least 2–3 times a week to maximise the benefits of this fatty acid. Fish high in Omega 3 are tuna, salmon, sardines, mackerel and herring. Both canned or fresh varieties of fish are suitable. If using canned fish, look for fish that is packed in water or brine rather than in oil. If using fresh fish, remember that smelling fish is the best way to determine whether it's fresh. To remove its scales, quickly run the whole fish under hot water. Keep fresh fish in the refrigerator in its own juices, covered with plastic wrap, for no more than one or two days. Cook fish and seafood by steaming, grilling, barbequing or baking in foil – methods that require no added fats. Fish is cooked when it turns white and flesh breaks open easily. The flesh of fish will hold together better if it's cooked with its skin attached. Remove skin in recipes that require fish to absorb sauce flavours.

FLOUR

Look for unbleached flours as these are free of chemicals. White flour has had the bran and husks removed, making it low in fibre. Wholemeal flour is high in fibre, contains nutrients and is a valuable protein source. It also absorbs more liquid, so if you're converting your favourite recipes add a little more liquid than specified in the recipe. Different flours have different tastes and textures that can change the flavour and texture of a recipe quite dramatically. It's necessary to sift flour for the best result in cooked recipes. There is a wide variety of flours from which to choose, including unbleached white, plain and self-raising; unbleached wholemeal, plain and self-raising; soy flour; rice flour; potato flour; and rye flour.

FRUIT

Fruit contains many vitamins and minerals and essential fibre, so it's recommended that you eat at least 2–3 servings of fruit every day. The best fruits (and the cheapest) are those that are in season. Store fruit in a cool place to maximise nutritional value.

GARLIC

This is a bulbous plant that is peeled, and then diced or crushed and added to soups, sauces, and meat and vegetable dishes to create a distinctive garlic flavour. It's not an essential ingredient so it can be omitted if you don't like it. Prepared garlic in small jars of vinegar can be purchased at supermarkets. You'll need to use a little more of this to get the same flavour as fresh garlic.

GELATIN/AGAR

Gelatin is a tasteless, odourless, pure protein powder (from animal sources) that when dissolved in liquid is used as a setting agent. Agar is a vegetable seaweed powder used by vegetarians for the same purpose. Agar is available from health food shops.

GINGER

A root vegetable that is peeled, diced and added to soups, sauces, stirfries and even dessert recipes to impart its delicate ginger flavour. Like garlic it can be found prepared in small jars of vinegar at supermarkets. It keeps for a long time in the refrigerator.

HERBS

Many different herbs are used to give a recipe its distinctive flavour. Herbs are an excellent salt substitute. Dried herbs can be used instead of fresh herbs by substituting 1 teaspoon of dried herbs for 1 tablespoon of fresh herbs. If you don't like the flavour of the herb used in a recipe, refer to the 'Herbs and spices' section in this book and experiment with other taste options.

ICE-CREAM

Make your own low-fat ice-cream with the recipe in this book or look for commercial varieties that have a fat content of less than 5 g per 100 g serve. You'll find delicious yoghurts and desserts in a variety of fruit flavours that are completely fat-free in supermarket freezers or at specialty ice-cream shops. Low-fat soft yoghurts can be served as a dessert alternative to ice-cream.

JAMS/SPREADS

Use the simple recipes in this book or choose from the sugar-free varieties available at supermarkets and health food shops.

LEGUMES

These include a variety of dried beans, lentils and peas. They are a good source of protein and as such are often used as a meat substitute. Legumes contain soluble fibre, which can help to lower cholesterol levels. The dried varieties need soaking overnight before cooking. The canned varieties need to be drained well before using and then run under cold water to eliminate excess sodium. Legumes are a versatile food that can be used in dips, soups, salads, pasta and rice dishes, as well as vegetarian burgers when combined with other vegetables.

MEAT

All lean meats are a good source of iron, zinc, niacin, thiamin, vitamins B6 and B12. Choose the best cuts of beef, lamb, chicken and pork and remove all visible fat (especially chicken skin) before cooking. Cook meat by grilling, baking, barbequing or using other cooking methods that require no added fat. When cooking meat always cook it a little longer on the first side, and then turn once only to cook the other side. Never serve chicken or pork rare, as both meats need to be cooked well to kill bacteria. A serving for an average adult is 90–125 g.

MILK

Use low-fat milk (containing 1 per cent fat) or skim milk powder mixed with water (almost fat-free). All fat-reduced milks are higher in calcium than full-fat milks. Soymilk can also be substituted for milk. *See also* soymilk.

NUTS/SEEDS

Almonds and sesame seeds are used in some recipes. They contain good levels of calcium and are highly nutritious. Both nuts and seeds are high in polyunsaturated fat, so use them in moderation in recipes or as snacks with fresh fruit.

OIL

Olive oil is used to wipe cooking utensils with a non-stick surface to avoid sticking and grapeseed oil is used in cake- and pastry-making. Grapeseed oil is a light oil with a bland taste that won't overpower other flavours. All oils are high in calories even though some contain more valuable fats than others. Use oil sparingly.

PASTA

Choose wholemeal pasta or pasta made from corn; avoid pasta made from eggs. If using pasta made from white flour, serve it with a mixed vegetable pasta sauce to provide the essential fibre. Leftover cooked pasta can be kept in the refrigerator and reheated as required, or it can be used in soups or made into delicious cold pasta salads.

PASTRY/FLAN BASES

Use the pastry recipes in this book or use filo pastry, which is available in supermarket freezers. Filo pastry is excellent for wrapping sweet or savoury ingredients that contain no fat. For sweet recipes, brush a mixture of 1 part water and 1 part apple juice concentrate between several sheets of filo pastry. For savoury recipes, brush a mixture of half a part olive oil and 1 part water or low-fat yoghurt. To make an excellent savoury flan base, mix 1 egg white with 2 cups of cooked, well-drained rice and press into a pie or quiche dish. Alternatively you could use wholegrain breadcrumbs processed with fresh herbs or salt-free tomato paste and press into a pie or flan dish. (Cook before adding filling.) If you're in a hurry, you can simply use wholegrain bread or Lebanese bread to cover a lightly oiled pie or flan base.

RICE
Brown rice contains approximately three times more fibre than white rice. It also takes a little longer to cook than white rice. If using white rice serve it with lots of high-fibre vegetables and high–fibre breads. Cooked rice keeps well in the refrigerator and reheats quickly to use as a side dish for main meals, in fried rice or tossed with cold leftover vegetables for a fast salad.

RICOTTA CHEESE
Ricotta cheese is an ideal full-fat cream substitute. Whip it smooth with some low–fat milk and use it as a white sauce in lasagne, or whip it smooth with a little apple juice concentrate and vanilla essence to make a delicious sweet cream to serve with fresh fruit. *See also* cheese.

SALAD DRESSINGS
Use the recipes in this book or look for oil-free and low-salt varieties available at supermarkets. A squeeze of lemon juice, a splash of gourmet herb vinegar or a little balsamic vinegar with crushed garlic, ginger or chives makes a quick and simple salad dressing option.

SKIM MILK POWDER
This is milk from which the moisture and fat have been removed. It's added to dry ingredients in baking or reconstituted to make a liquid by adding water.

SOYMILK

This is milk made from soya beans. It's an excellent source of protein and contains phytoestrogens vital for the prevention of breast cancer and heart disease. Most varieties of soymilk have the same calcium content as milk. They tend to be higher in fat than milk, so be careful to choose a low-fat variety or dilute full-fat soymilk (4 parts water to 1 part soymilk) to make it lower in fat. Soymilk is an excellent alternative to regular milk for those with a lactose intolerance and can easily be substituted in all recipes using regular milk.
See also milk.

SOY SAUCE

An almost black, thin sauce made from fermented soya beans. It enhances the flavour of vegetable, meat, fish and rice dishes. Use the low-salt variety only. Low-salt soy sauce with chopped garlic, chopped fresh ginger or chopped fresh chilli makes a great dipping sauce for vegetable crudités.

SPICES

A variety of spices are used in the recipes in this book for added flavour. Increase or decrease the amount used in a recipe depending on your particular taste. If you don't like the flavour of the spice used in a recipe, refer to the 'Herbs and spices' section in this book and experiment with other taste options.

SPROUTS

Keep some sprouts (alfalfa, mung beans or lentil sprouts) in the refrigerator. They make an ideal quick snack on biscuits or in sandwiches, a garnish for soups, a topping on vegetarian pizza or baked potatoes, and an ingredient in all salads. They're rich in nearly all vitamins and minerals and are a good source of protein and enzymes.

STOCK (chicken, beef, fish)
Use chicken carcasses or beef bones, fish scraps and
seafood shells. Add water, onions, vegetables, herbs, ginger
and/or garlic and simmer for at least two hours. Strain and
cool. Use as required.

STOCK (vegetable)
There are commercial varieties available but check that
the sodium content is not too high. Make your own
vegetable stock at home by using chopped vegetables,
clean vegetable peelings and onion skins. Add water,
chopped onions, herbs, ginger and/or garlic and simmer
for at least two hours. Strain and cool. Use as required.

TOFU
This is a bland-tasting soya bean curd. It's made by adding
a natural coagulant such as lemon juice to soymilk. Curds
are created, the excess milk is drained off, and the curds
are pressed into blocks to further remove all liquid. It has
an excellent protein and calcium content, and is both low
in fat and cholesterol free. Tofu can be substituted for
cottage cheese or ricotta cheese, and can be used in salads,
and in sweet and savoury recipes. It's great chopped into
squares and added to a vegetable stirfry.

TOMATO PASTE
This is a concentrated purée of tomatoes. You can make
your own by peeling and seeding the tomatoes, chopping
them finely and cooking them until they reduce and
thicken. Alternatively you can use salt-free commercial
varieties.

VEGETABLES
Like fruit, vegetables contain lots of vitamins, minerals,
folic acid and fibre. It's recommended that we eat at least
5 servings of vegetables – two-thirds raw and one-third
cooked – in our daily diet. One serve equals half a cup

cooked vegetables or 1 cup raw salad or three-quarters cup vegetable juice. Vegetables are best steamed in their own moisture or with just a minimum of added water. Don't allow vegetables to stand in water before cooking as water leaches out the vegetables' vital nutrients. Because avocados are high in monounsaturated fat they're best eaten on a meat-free day. Frozen vegetables can be used instead of fresh vegetables occasionally. They are picked fresh, then frozen and packaged quickly to maintain nutritional value. Always simmer frozen vegetables rather than boil them rapidly so as to retain maximum nutrients.

YEAST
Baker's yeast in granulated form is used in the bread recipes in this book. It should be stored in a dry, cool place in an airtight container.

YOGHURT
Make your own low-fat yoghurt from the recipe in this book and add sweet or savoury ingredients when the yoghurt has set. Alternatively look for commercial varieties that have a fat content of less than 5 g per 100 g serve. The sugar content of low-fat yoghurts and full-fat varieties is usually the same. Look for brands that have real fruit ingredients. Yoghurt contains live lactobacillus acidophilus, which restores the balance of good bacteria in the gut. Yoghurt makes a good base for low-fat ice-cream, creamy salad dressings, dips, and savoury and sweet sauces.

Herbs
and spices

Herbs

BALM/LEMON BALM

This herb has a very strong lemon scent. The leaves are oval in shape and crinkly like spearmint.

Use Fresh leaves are floated on top of cool drinks and are also delicious when added – chopped – to fruit salad. They give a lemon tang to a tossed green salad. Fresh or dried lemon balm may be infused in a teapot to make a refreshing pick-me-up drink.

BASIL

Sweet basil has soft, light green leaves; bush basil has much smaller leaves. When broken and rubbed with the fingers, the foliage has a spicy aroma like cloves. Sweet basil has a slightly stronger perfume than bush basil.

Use Fresh or dry leaves can be used with eggplant and capsicum, in vegetable soups and Italian dishes, to season tomatoes and make tomato sauce. The fresh leaves are excellent in a tossed salad, potato salad, rice salad, and cooked green bean salad. Basil is one of the most useful herbs.

BAY LEAVES

The sweet bay is an aromatic evergreen with glossy leaves. It's essential in a bouquet garni: a tied bunch of bay leaves, thyme and parsley used to flavour sauces, stews and so on.

Use Bay leaves can be used to flavour marinades, stocks, soups, poultry and fish dishes. They may be used fresh or dried, but should be kept in an airtight container.

BORAGE

This herb has broad, hairy leaves with a cucumber flavour.

Use When chopped very finely, borage leaves make fillings for sandwiches and can be added to tossed salads. The whole young leaves can be used in cool drinks.

CARAWAY

This is a herb with frond-like leaves. The pungent seeds are rich in aromatic oils, and are prized for their use in cooking and as an aid to digestion. Store seeds in an airtight container.

Use Caraway seeds are commonly used in bread, especially rye bread. They flavour vegetables such as cabbage, carrots and cauliflower, as well as soups and stewed and baked fruits such as apples and pears.

CHERVIL

The foliage of this herb resembles a fine-leafed parsley and has a delicate aniseed taste.

Use The chopped fresh or dried leaves go into the classic 'fines herbes', which comprises equal proportions of chervil, tarragon, parsley and chives. Put in mashed potatoes, green salads and white sauces for fish or poultry.

CHIVES

Onion chives have a round, hollow leaf with a mild onion flavour. Garlic chives have a flat leaf that is broader than onion chives and not so dark green in colour. The flavour is mildly garlicky. Chives are very easy to grow in a small garden or pot in a well-watered, sunny position.

Use Chopped chives go into salads and cream cheese, and can be used as a garnish for baked potatoes, soups, fish and sauces.

CORIANDER

Coriander has lacy, feathery foliage. Ripe coriander seeds are slightly oval, small, beige in colour and have a spicy aroma. This herb is very popular in Asian-style recipes.

Use The ground seeds are used to give a tang to fish, poultry and meat dishes. They also flavour cakes, biscuits, pastries and bread. Sprinkle a little ground coriander over apples, pears and peaches while baking. Just a pinch is enough to flavour eggplant and capsicum.

DILL

This herb has delicate, dark green aromatic foliage. Its seeds have a pungently dry aromatic flavour akin to aniseed.

Use The foliage, either the fresh chopped leaves or the dried crumbled leaves, flavours dips, spreads, sauces, salad dressings, coleslaw, tossed green salads, potato salad, fish and rice. Sprinkle on vegetables lightly. The seeds flavour pickles, chutney, coleslaw, creamed fish, meat loaf, potato salad, cottage cheese, cabbage, cauliflower and cucumber. Dill is an excellent herb used with seafood.

FENNEL

The fresh foliage of this herb is chopped finely and sprinkled over fish while cooking, or the whole leaves are used as a stuffing for fish.

Use The seeds, which have digestive properties, go into pastries, bread, and fish and meat dishes, and can be added to steamed cabbage while cooking. They are excellent in beetroot or potato salads.

LOVAGE

A European herb with tasty leaves.

Use The tasty lovage leaves give flavour to soups, vegetables and salads.

MARJORAM

Marjoram and oregano are from the same mint family and are often (incorrectly) used interchangeably.

Use Marjoram is great in savoury sauces, pasta and rice dishes, some meat dishes and pizza. It's also used with tomatoes, eggplant, capsicum and zucchini.

MINT

This is a refreshing herb with a cool, clean flavour. It's best grown in a controlled area as it grows rampant.

Use Excellent with citrus fruit, new potatoes, peas, carrots and tomatoes, and in cool drinks, tomato sauces, mint sauce, and orange and onion salad.

OREGANO

Oregano is simply the wild form of marjoram, and has arguably a more pungent flavour than marjoram.

Use Commonly used with pasta, rice, tomatoes, eggplant, capsicum, zucchini, and in pizzas, savoury sauces, and some meat dishes.

PARSLEY

An old favourite for many reasons. Firstly, it has attractive leaves perfect for garnishes. Secondly, it has a pleasing taste and contains many health-giving vitamins and minerals. Thirdly, it is an excellent breath deodoriser to combat garlic and onion odours. It combines beautifully with chopped chives. Every garden deserves a parsley patch.

Use The leaves can be used as a garnish or chopped in soups, over salads, vegetables, pasta dishes, rice and mashed potatoes.

ROSEMARY

A well-known 'roasting' herb with pungent leaves.

Use Chopped fresh or dried leaves are wonderful in stuffing for meat or chicken. Rosemary leaves can be added to potato pastry, spinach, carrots, zucchini and eggplant. Add a large bunch to a baking dish when roasting beef or lamb.

SAGE

Sage is one of the ingredients found in mixed herbs; the others being marjoram and thyme.

Use This herb is used with onions to make stuffing. It's also used to season breadcrumbs to be used with chicken or fish.

SALAD BURNET

This herb has soft, serrated fern-like leaves which have a mild cucumber flavour.

Use The leaves go into tossed salads and iced drinks, and are delicious finely chopped in herb sandwiches.

TARRAGON

This is a strong-flavoured herb, and so a little goes a long way. French tarragon is recommended for culinary use; it does not set seeds. Tarragon must be dried quickly to keep its colour and flavour.

Use The spicy, somewhat tart taste of the leaves gives a piquant flavour to poultry and fish. Add to a wine vinegar and keep aside for a dressing.

THYME

Garden thyme is the variety most used in cooking. It can be picked fresh throughout the year.

Use Thyme seasons meat loaf, rissoles, stews, soups and strongly flavoured vegetables like onions, steamed cabbage, swede, turnips and parsnips. It also makes an excellent herbal tea.

WINTER SAVOURY

The foliage of this herb has a peppery flavour. It dries easily and will keep its true flavour for a time if stored in an airtight container.

Use The peppery flavour is perfect in rissoles, savoury mince, beans and pea soups, sauces and salads. The chopped leaves can be sprinkled over cooked marrows, zucchini, squash and beans.

Spices

ALLSPICE

A spice with an aroma similar to a combination of cinnamon, cloves and nutmeg. The flavour is strong, so it should be used sparingly.

Use Chutneys, relish, marinades, cakes and steamed puddings can be flavoured with allspice.

CAYENNE

A ground spice of the chilli pepper family.

Use This spice should be used sparingly to flavour seafood and sauces. It can also be an interesting addition to a basic coleslaw.

CHILLIES

Chillies come whole-dried or finely ground.

Use This spice can be used to add flavour to curries, chutneys and rice dishes.

CINNAMON

This spice is the bark of a tree native to Sri Lanka. It's presented in a rolled-up quill form or finely ground. It's arguably the most popular of spices.

Use Cinnamon adds flavour to rice dishes, curries, cooked fruits such as apples, apricots or pears, cakes and steamed puddings. Cinnamon and orange juice added to a natural yoghurt makes a refreshing summer dessert.

CLOVES

A spice with a powerful flavour that should be used very sparingly.

Use Whole cloves or ground cloves are great added to cooking apples and pears, chutneys, steamed puddings, dried fruits and some vegetable dishes.

GINGER (ground)

This spice gives a spicy, warm flavour.

Use When cooking meat and vegetable dishes, ginger is usually teamed with other spices such as garam masala, garlic powder, cumin powder and cardamom. A little goes a long way so it should be used sparingly in desserts, cakes and steamed puddings.

MACE

Mace is the outer casing of nutmeg. It has a flavour similar to nutmeg but is slightly more refined. Half a teaspoon of mace is equal to a quarter of a teaspoon of nutmeg.

Use This spice can be used to flavour soups, vegetable casseroles, sauces and stuffing.

MUSTARD

This spice comes in seed or powder form. Its flavour is pleasantly pungent.

Use Mustard is used to add flavour to white sauces, mayonnaise or vegetable dishes.

NUTMEG

Nutmeg is most suitably used fresh and grated to capture its true flavour.

Use This is a widely used spice in hot or cold drinks and spicy or sweet dishes. Try it with fish, veal, spinach, carrots, cakes and cooked fruit.

PAPRIKA

This spice is used for its flavour and colour. It's the ground seed of the sweet pepper and ranges from mild to sweet to mildly hot.

Use The bright red colour of this spice immediately adds warmth and interest to any dish. It flavours chicken, vegetables, fish and sauces.

Starters

Brown rice stuffed tomatoes Serves 8

8 medium tomatoes
1 cup cooked brown rice
1 onion, finely chopped
$^2/_3$ cup currants
2 tablespoons chopped pine nuts
  or almonds

2 tablespoons chopped fresh mint
black pepper
$^1/_2$ cup wholemeal breadcrumbs

Slice tops from tomatoes and scoop out pulp with a metal spoon. Remove seeds and roughly chop remaining flesh.

Combine chopped tomato with remaining ingredients – except breadcrumbs. Place tomato cases in a baking dish. Spoon mixture into tomato cases. Sprinkle breadcrumbs over each tomato, and bake at 170°C for 20 minutes or until breadcrumbs are browned. Serve with salad greens or freshly cooked asparagus spears.

Carrot dip Makes 2 cups

1 bunch baby carrots, washed and
  chopped
1 teaspoon fresh lemon juice

1–2 tablespoons fresh orange juice
$^1/_2$–1 teaspoon nutmeg
1 cup cottage cheese or tofu

Place carrots in a steamer. Steam until tender. Purée all ingredients until smooth.

Chargrilled vegetables with fresh tomato purée

Serves 4

2 parsnips
4 carrots
2 zucchini
1 red capsicum, seeded
1 green capsicum, seeded
1 yellow capsicum, seeded

FRESH TOMATO PURÉE
1 kg peeled, seeded and chopped
  ripe tomatoes
2 bay leaves
6 peppercorns
6 whole cloves
1 tablespoon apple juice
  concentrate
$1/4$ cup water or white wine
black pepper
pinch salt

Cut all vegetables into long strips of similar size. Heat a non-stick or lightly oiled pan (a chargrill pan is preferable). Cook vegetables on both sides.

To make the tomato purée, place all purée ingredients – except pepper and salt – in a saucepan and bring to the boil. Reduce heat and simmer, covered, until tomatoes are very soft. Push tomatoes through a sieve and discard bay leaves, peppercorns and cloves. Season with pepper and salt. Place vegetables evenly on four separate plates and spoon tomato purée over the top.

Cheesy
pear with balsamic fruit salad Serves 1

$^1/_2$ cup fruit salad (strawberries,
   apples, cucumber, kiwi fruit,
   grapes, peaches), finely diced
1 tablespoon balsamic vinegar

$^1/_2$ ripe pear, seeded
2 heaped tablespoons cottage
   cheese or mashed tofu

Marinate fruit salad in vinegar. Fill pear half with cottage cheese or tofu and garnish with balsamic fruit salad.

Fresh
peach or pear appetiser Serves 4

2 large peaches or pears, stoned,
   and halved
4 lettuce leaves
125 g cottage cheese or mashed
   tofu

1 tablespoon chopped fresh chives
90 g finely chopped walnuts
30 g peeled and grated fresh
   ginger

Place each peach or pear half onto a lettuce leaf. Combine remaining ingredients and mix well. Fill each peach or pear cavity with the mixture.

Frozen pineapple cocktail Serves 4–6

1 x 450 g can crushed
  unsweetened pineapple
300 ml fresh orange juice
300 ml fresh grapefruit juice

1–2 tablespoons apple juice
  concentrate
chopped fresh mint (for garnish)

Mix all ingredients – except mint – and freeze until just mushy. Spoon into stemmed glasses and garnish with mint.

Note This is an excellent refresher to start a meal. For a more tart, refreshing cocktail leave out the apple juice concentrate.

Salmon dip Makes 2 cups

1 x 450 g can salmon, well drained
225 g cottage cheese or ricotta
  cheese or tofu
3 tablespoons salt-free tomato
  paste

1 tablespoon fresh lemon juice
black pepper
3 shallots, very finely chopped

Blend all ingredients – except shallots. Fold in shallots. Serve as a dip with vegetable crudités or a selection of fresh wholegrain or rye bread with salad greens.

Savoury crepes

Makes 4 large or 6 small crepes

1/2 cup unbleached wholemeal
  plain flour
1 teaspoon dry mustard
1/2 teaspoon dill
1/2 teaspoon basil or chives or
  parsley or oregano

1 cup low-fat milk or low-fat
  soymilk
2 egg whites
filling (see below)

Blend all ingredients and let stand for 30 minutes. Pour mixture onto a hot, lightly oiled non-stick pan and quickly spread mixture over the base of pan. (The mixture should spread very thinly so that the crepes are paper-thin.) As bubbles appear, turn crepes over and brown on the other side. Remove crepes to a sheet of non-stick baking paper. Crepes can be cooked and kept warm until required.

Note To store cooked crepes, layer them between sheets of non-stick baking paper and refrigerate or wrap in plastic and freeze.

FILLINGS
Asparagus filling

1 quantity white sauce (see recipe
  on page 152)
250 g cooked chopped asparagus

1–2 teaspoons chopped fresh
  chervil
1 teaspoon lemon juice

Heat white sauce. Add asparagus, chervil and lemon juice. Spread mixture over crepe and roll up.

Chicken and tomato filling

$^1/_2$ cup chopped shallots

1 cup sliced mushrooms

1 x 425 g can salt-free tomatoes and juice

2 tablespoons salt-free tomato paste

2 cups diced cooked chicken (no skin)

1 cup cooked well-drained spinach

black pepper

Place the first four ingredients into a saucepan and cook until mixture thickens and reduces. Add chicken and spinach. Cook to warm through. Season with pepper. Spread mixture over crepe and roll up.

Fish filling

1 quantity white sauce (see recipe on page 152)

250 g steamed and flaked fish fillet

1 tablespoon dry sherry or fresh orange juice

1 tablespoon finely chopped fresh dill

squeeze of fresh lemon

ground black pepper

sprigs of fresh dill (for garnish)

Combine all ingredients – except dill – and heat through. Spread mixture over crepe and roll up. Squeeze lemon over crepe, sprinkle with pepper and garnish with sprigs of fresh dill.

Mushroom and walnut filling

500 g peeled and sliced mushrooms

$^1/_4$ cup chicken stock (see recipe on page 40)

$^1/_4$ cup finely chopped walnuts

2 tablespoons water

2 teaspoons cornflour

black pepper

2 tablespoons finely chopped fresh parsley

Cook mushrooms gently in chicken stock for 3 minutes. Add walnuts and simmer for a further 5 minutes. Combine water and cornflour and mix to a paste. Stir this into mushroom mixture and cook until thickened. Season with pepper. Spread mushroom mixture over crepe, sprinkle with fresh parsley and roll up.

Savoury
rock melons <small>Serves 6</small>

3 small rock melons
4 tablespoons fresh lemon juice
$^3/_4$ cup low-fat yoghurt
1 tablespoon lemon rind
1 tablespoon finely chopped fresh
  basil
black pepper
1 teaspoon peeled and finely
  grated fresh ginger

2 cups chopped cooked chicken
  (no skin)
1 cup green grapes
$^1/_2$ red capsicum, seeded and
  finely diced
$^1/_2$ cup celery, threaded and finely
  diced
toasted almond slivers

Halve the rock melons and remove seeds. Pour a little of the lemon juice over the top. Combine remaining ingredients – except almond slivers. Fill melons with mixture and sprinkle with almond slivers. You might like to sit rock melons on a bed of lettuce leaves so they don't move about.

Sorrel trout terrine   Serves 4

1½ cups sorrel or spinach leaves, blanched and well drained
500 g cooked mashed trout flesh or 1 x 425 g can red salmon, well drained
1 cup fresh rye or wholegrain breadcrumbs
2 egg whites
2 Granny Smith apples, peeled and grated
1 tablespoon fresh lemon juice
1–2 tablespoons green peppercorns
¼ cup low-fat yoghurt

Place a single layer of sorrel or spinach leaves, slightly overlapping, in the base of a 10 x 20-cm glass terrine. Combine remaining ingredients and place half the fish mixture over the sorrel or spinach leaves, pressing down firmly. Arrange another layer of sorrel or spinach leaves on top of fish mixture. Repeat with another layer of fish and sorrel or spinach leaves.

Cover with foil and place in a baking dish containing 2 cm of warm water. Bake in lower half of oven at 160°C for approximately 30–40 minutes. Allow to cool and refrigerate overnight. Remove terrine from dish. Cut into slices and serve with salad greens.

Tomato
sorbet Serves 6–8

1 quantity fresh tomato purée (see recipe on page 29)
1 cup fresh orange juice
1 cup chicken stock (see recipe on page 40)
few drops Tabasco
1 tablespoon dry sherry
1 teaspoon finely grated orange rind

1 teaspoon peeled and finely grated fresh ginger
1 egg white
1 tablespoon finely chopped fresh coriander
sprigs of fresh coriander (for garnish)

Purée all ingredients – except egg white and coriander – until well combined. Pour ingredients into a metal freezer tray. Freeze until mushy, stirring occasionally with a fork.

Transfer to a bowl. Beat egg white until stiff and fold into tomato mixture along with coriander. Return immediately to freezer tray and freeze until firm. (Alternatively, combine ingredients, pour into an ice-cream maker and follow freezing instructions.) Spoon sorbet into goblets and garnish with sprigs of fresh coriander.

Soups

Almond
soup Serves 4–6

1 cup ground blanched almonds
4 cups low-fat milk
1 leek, washed and finely chopped
1 celery heart, finely diced

pinch cayenne pepper
$1/4$ cup toasted flaked almonds
  (for garnish)
pinch ground nutmeg (for garnish)

Place almonds, milk, leek and celery in a saucepan and simmer over low heat until vegetables are soft. Purée. Season with cayenne pepper. Soup may be served hot or well chilled. Garnish with almonds and nutmeg, and serve.

Bean
soup with parsley Serves 6–8

200 g haricot beans
1 onion, diced
2 carrots, chopped
2 leeks, washed and chopped
2 sticks celery, chopped
1 x 425 g can salt-free tomatoes
  and juice

2 litres chicken stock (see recipe
  on page 40)
black pepper
6 tablespoons chopped fresh
  parsley

Soak beans in water for 3–4 hours. Drain well and remove any beans that float to the surface. Cover with fresh water and cook slowly until beans are tender. Drain beans, reserving the cooking liquid.

Combine all remaining ingredients – except pepper and parsley – in a large saucepan. Cover and cook for 1 hour. Remove lid, add beans and bean liquid, and cook for a further 30 minutes with lid off. Soup will thicken as it cooks and reduces. Add pepper to taste, then stir in chopped parsley.

OPPOSITE: *Parsley and vegetable soup (see page 43).*

Carrot and parsnip soup   Serves 4

1 large onion, diced
2 sticks celery and leaves,
   chopped
1 large parsnip, grated
2–3 large carrots, grated
1 litre water or vegetable stock
   (see recipe on page 45)

2 bay leaves
black pepper
$^1/_2$ teaspoon thyme
extra black pepper
chopped fresh herbs of your
   choice

Combine all ingredients – except extra pepper and herbs –
in a saucepan. Bring to the boil. Simmer, covered, for 1
hour. Purée 2 cups of the vegetables and return to soup.
Add extra pepper and chopped fresh herbs of your choice.

Carrot and turnip soup with coriander

Serves 4–6

250 g chopped baby carrots
250 g peeled and chopped turnips
1 litre chicken stock (see recipe on
   page 40)
black pepper
2 teaspoons ground coriander

1 teaspoon ground cumin
$^1/_2$ cup low-fat yoghurt (for
   garnish)
1 tablespoon finely chopped fresh
   coriander leaves (for garnish)

Combine all ingredients – except yoghurt and coriander –
and cook, covered, until vegetables are tender. Purée. Serve
garnished with yoghurt and coriander.

OPPOSITE: *Pancakes
with savoury
chicken filling
(see page 85).*

Chicken stock Makes 1¹/₂ litres

2 litres water
1 kg chicken bones, carcass or
  fresh meat

¹/₂ lemon
celery leaves
black pepper

Combine all ingredients in a large saucepan. Bring to the boil. Simmer for 1 hour and strain. Store in the refrigerator.

Note Chicken stock can be frozen.

Chilled tomato soup with basil Serves 4

1 onion, diced
500–700 g peeled, seeded and
  chopped ripe tomatoes
¹/₄ cup fresh orange juice
2¹/₂ cups chicken stock (see recipe
  above)

black pepper
pinch salt
3 tablespoons chopped fresh basil

Cook onion, tomatoes and orange juice until all moisture has been absorbed. Add stock, pepper and salt to taste and simmer for a further 15 minutes. Purée in a blender, adjust seasoning, then cool and chill well. Stir in basil 10 minutes before serving.

Chinese chicken stock Makes 1½ litres

1 kg chicken or chicken pieces
2 litres water
3-cm piece fresh green ginger,
  peeled and sliced

4 peppercorns
1 onion (not peeled), chopped
3 sprigs of fresh parsley

Combine all ingredients in a large saucepan. Bring to the boil then simmer for 1½ hours. Cool and strain.

Note Chicken stock can be frozen.

Creamy corn soup Serves 4–6

2 litres chicken stock (see recipe
  on page 40)
3 large potatoes, peeled and diced
1 onion, diced
1 cup chopped celery leaves

2 cups fresh or well-drained
  canned corn kernels
1–2 cups low-fat milk
black pepper

Combine stock, potatoes, onion, celery leaves and corn. Bring to the boil. Simmer, covered, until potato and corn are tender. Purée and return to a clean saucepan. Add milk depending on how thick you require the soup to be. Reheat, but do not boil. Season with pepper to taste.

Note For a milk-free soup, substitute extra chicken stock and/or a little white wine for milk.

Gazpacho

Serves 4–6

500 g peeled, seeded and
  chopped ripe tomatoes
1 small onion, finely diced
1 small green capsicum, seeded
  and diced
1 clove garlic, crushed

$^1/_2$ cup dry white wine
1–2 teaspoons fresh lemon juice
black pepper
pinch salt
1 x 40 g can salt-free tomato juice
cucumber slices (for garnish)

Blend the first five ingredients. Add lemon juice, pepper
and salt to taste. Dilute the soup to your desired
consistency with the tomato juice. Chill well before
serving. Garnish with slices of cucumber.

Minestrone

Serves 4–6

2 cloves garlic, crushed
1 large onion, chopped
2 litres chicken or vegetable stock
  (see recipes on pages 40 and 45)
2 large carrots, diced
3 sticks celery and leaves,
  chopped
1 large potato, peeled and
  chopped
3 small zucchini, chopped
10 green beans, chopped

$^1/_2$ cup sliced mushrooms
2 x 425 g cans salt-free tomatoes
  and juice
black pepper
1 teaspoon marjoram
1 cup chopped cooked chicken (no
  skin)
3 cups cooked haricot beans
$^1/_2$ cup cooked brown rice or
  $^1/_2$ cup cooked wholemeal
  macaroni

Combine all ingredients – except chicken, haricot beans,
and rice or macaroni – in a large saucepan. Cover and
cook for 1 hour. Add chicken, haricot beans, and rice or
macaroni, and cook for a further 5–10 minutes or until
these ingredients are heated through.

Parsley and vegetable soup Serves 4

1 onion, diced
2 large carrots, chopped
½ parsnip, chopped
1 large potato, peeled and
  chopped

l litre chicken stock (see recipe on
  page 40)
black pepper
¾ cup finely chopped fresh
  parsley

Add vegetables to stock with pepper to taste and cook
over gentle heat for 30–40 minutes or until vegetables are
tender. Purée. Stir through the parsley, adding extra pepper
as required.

Pumpkin and tomato soup with basil Serves 4

500 g peeled and cubed pumpkin
250 g peeled, seeded and chopped
  ripe tomatoes
250 g chopped carrots
1.5 litres chicken stock (see recipe
  on page 40)

1 onion, diced
2 teaspoons basil
black pepper
2 tablespoons chopped fresh basil
2 teaspoons apple juice
  concentrate

Combine all ingredients – except basil and apple juice
concentrate – in a saucepan and bring to the boil, covered.
Turn down heat and simmer until vegetables are tender.
Purée. Stir in basil and apple juice concentrate just
before serving.

Summer soup Serves 4

500 g peeled, seeded and
  chopped ripe tomatoes
1 cucumber, peeled and seeded
1 clove garlic, crushed
$1/2$ glass dry sherry

black pepper
4 tablespoons low-fat yoghurt
$1/4$ cup finely chopped fresh
  parsley

Blend the first five ingredients until very smooth. Chill for
several hours. Before serving, stir in yoghurt and parsley.

Tomato soup with croutons Serves 4–6

500 g peeled, seeded and
  chopped ripe tomatoes
$1/2$ onion, diced
1 medium potato, peeled and
  diced
2 cups water or vegetable stock
  (see recipe on page 45)
black pepper
squeeze of fresh lemon
sprig of fresh basil

CROUTONS
2 slices wholemeal bread
$1/2$ cup ricotta cheese
cayenne pepper

Place ingredients in a saucepan and bring to the boil.
Simmer, covered, until vegetables are tender. Purée.
To make the croutons, spread bread with ricotta cheese
and sprinkle with cayenne pepper. Bake at 190°C for
10 minutes and cut into croutons. Add to soup just
before serving.

Vegetable stock

Makes 1.5 litres

2 litres water
potatoes
carrots
onions
celery head
celery leaves
spinach
swede
turnip
parsnip
tomatoes

EXTRAS
$^1/_2$ lemon
black pepper
$^1/_4$ cup dry sherry
$^1/_4$ cup fresh orange juice
$^1/_4$ cup tomato juice or 4
    tablespoons tomato purée

All or any of these vegetables in a combination would be suitable to make a vegetable stock. Chop vegetables, cover with water and add any extras. Bring to the boil. Simmer, covered, for 1–2 hours. When cold, strain.

Note The remaining vegetable pulp can be used to thicken soups, pasta sauces or casseroles. Purée and set aside. The strained stock can be frozen.

Vichyssoise

Serves 6

4 cups chicken stock (see recipe on page 40)

4 medium potatoes, peeled and chopped

3 medium onions, diced

3 leeks, washed and sliced

1 tablespoon finely grated orange rind

$^1/_2$ teaspoon marjoram

2 tablespoons chopped fresh parsley

150 ml low-fat yoghurt

black pepper

chopped fresh herbs of your choice

Place all ingredients – except yoghurt, pepper and herbs – in a saucepan. Bring to the boil. Cover and simmer until vegetables are soft. Purée. Chill well. Stir in yoghurt, pepper and herbs before serving.

Salads

Alfalfa sprout salad Serves 4

3 sticks celery, diagonally sliced
1 cucumber, peeled, halved, seeded and sliced
6 shallots, diagonally sliced
10 button mushrooms, thinly sliced
1 red apple, cored, peeled and cut into strips

2 tomatoes, peeled, seeded and chopped
1 cup alfalfa sprouts
2 tablespoons chopped fresh herbs of your choice
juice of $1/2$ lemon

Combine all ingredients. Toss lightly and refrigerate.

Banana and celery salad Serves 4

1 lettuce
4 bananas (not too ripe), peeled and sliced
$1/4$ cup fresh lemon juice combined with $1/2$ cup water

3 cups diagonally sliced celery
$1/4$ cup chopped fresh chives
1 cup low-fat yoghurt
black pepper
$1/4$ cup sesame seeds or pine nuts

Set aside 4 crisp lettuce cups. Shred the remaining lettuce finely. Soak bananas in lemon juice and water for 5 minutes. Drain well. Combine bananas, shredded lettuce and celery in a bowl.

Mix chives, yoghurt and pepper. Add this mixture to lettuce, bananas and celery and toss well. Spoon equal amounts into each lettuce leaf. Sprinkle with sesame seeds or pine nuts.

Beetroot mould Serves 4–6

6 medium beetroot, thoroughly
  washed
2 teaspoons gelatine
2 tablespoons hot water
2 tablespoons fresh lemon juice

1 cup low-fat yoghurt
$^1/_2$ cup finely chopped fresh
  parsley
1 orange, sliced (for garnish)

Cook beetroot and reserve cooking liquid. When beetroot have cooled, peel, roughly chop and purée. If the mixture is too dry, add a small amount of beetroot cooking liquid or a dash of white wine. Set aside.

Dissolve gelatine in hot water and add lemon juice. Stir the gelatine mixture through the beetroot. Add yoghurt and parsley. Pour mixture into mould and refrigerate until set. Cut into portions and garnish with slices of orange.

Cabbage salad with dill Serves 4–6

$^1/_4$ head hard white cabbage,
  shredded
1 small cucumber, peeled, seeded
  and sliced
8 spring onions, chopped
1 tablespoon white-wine vinegar

2 tablespoons fresh lemon juice
2 tablespoons chopped fresh dill
black pepper
$^1/_4$ cup tangy yoghurt dressing or
  2 tablespoons low-fat mayonnaise
  (see recipes on pages 144 and 149)

Combine all ingredients. Toss lightly and refrigerate.

Carrot
and raisin salad Serves 4

1 cup raisins
$^1/_4$ cup fresh lemon or orange
  juice

3 cups grated carrot
2 tablespoons finely chopped
  fresh mint

Soak raisins in lemon or orange juice until plump. Add to carrot and mint and toss well.

Chicken
caraway coleslaw Serves 4–6

2 cups chopped cooked chicken
  (no skin)
1 tablespoon caraway seeds
$^1/_2$ cabbage, finely shredded

$^1/_2$ cup oil-free dressing
6 spring onions, diagonally sliced
1 green capsicum, seeded and
  finely sliced

Combine all ingredients and toss lightly. Chill well.

Coleslaw
Serves 6–8

6 cups finely shredded cabbage
1 cup parcooked or raw thinly
  sliced green beans
1 cup cooked green peas
$^1/_2$ cup finely chopped celery
$^1/_4$ cup corn kernels
$^1/_2$ cup grated carrot

$^1/_2$ cup seeded and finely chopped
  red capsicum
1 cup finely chopped fresh chives
pinch cayenne pepper
black pepper
1 quantity tangy yoghurt dressing
  (see recipe on page 144)

Combine all ingredients and toss well.

Cucumber
salad mould Serves 4

½ cucumber, peeled, seeded and
  chopped
1 orange, peeled
½ lemon, peeled
½ small onion, chopped
2 sprigs of fresh parsley
2 teaspoons gelatine

2 tablespoons hot water
1½ cups mixed grated vegetables
  (carrot, cucumber, radish, green
  and red capsicum)
black pepper
cucumber slices (for garnish)

Juice cucumber, orange, lemon, onion and parsley. Make
up to 1¼ cups with water, stock or white wine if
necessary. Dissolve gelatine in hot water, stir into juice and
add grated vegetables. Season with pepper to taste. Pour
mixture into a ring mould and refrigerate to set. Remove
from mould and garnish with slices of fresh cucumber.

Garden
salad Serves 4–6

1 cup cooked broccoli heads
1 cup cooked cauliflower heads
6 black olives, finely chopped
1 cup cherry tomatoes
½ Spanish onion, diced

2 tablespoons chopped fresh basil
½ cup chopped spring onion
2 teaspoons balsamic vinegar
black pepper

Combine all ingredients and toss lightly.

Hot peachy coleslaw   Serves 6–8

$^1/_2$ small cabbage, finely shredded
2 apples, cored and finely diced
2 Spanish onions, finely diced
4 peaches, peeled and chopped

DRESSING
$^1/_2$ cup fresh orange juice
1 tablespoon tahini
1 teaspoon grated fresh ginger
1 teaspoon curry paste
$^1/_4$ teaspoon chilli paste

Combine all salad ingredients. Then combine all dressing ingredients. Toss salad lightly in dressing.

Note Add 1 cup chopped pecans for a crunchy variation.

Island surprise pasta salad   Serves 4–6

1 green zucchini, cooked and chopped into rounds
1 yellow zucchini, cooked and chopped into rounds
1 carrot, cooked and chopped into rounds
2 sticks celery, chopped
$^1/_2$ cup chopped walnuts

$^1/_4$ cup chopped macadamia nuts
1 tablespoon sesame seeds
1 orange, peeled and chopped
1 cup fresh pineapple chunks
1 cup cooked cold soyaroni noodles
1 tablespoon capers

Combine all ingredients. If salad is a little dry, add a squeeze of fresh orange.

Orange and mint salad   Serves 4-6

1 large salad or odourless onion,
   sliced
1 cucumber, peeled and sliced

4 oranges, peeled and sliced
$^1/_2$ cup chopped fresh mint leaves
1 cup white-wine vinegar

Arrange layers of onion, cucumber then orange
alternatively in a bowl. Sprinkle each layer of orange with
mint before repeating. Pour enough vinegar over to cover.
Cover with plastic wrap and chill prior to serving.

Parsley and fennel tomato salad   Serves 4-6

2 bunches spring onions, chopped
125 g finely diced fennel root
400 g peeled, seeded and
   chopped ripe tomatoes
$^3/_4$ cup coarsely chopped fresh
   parsley

$^1/_3$ cup coarsely chopped fresh
   mint
2 tablespoons fresh lemon juice
black pepper

Combine all ingredients and toss well.

Potato salad (baked) Serves 4–6

500 g washed new potatoes
1 salad onion, diced
1 green capsicum, seeded and
  diced
1 red capsicum, seeded and diced
1 cup chopped celery

1 cup grated carrot
black pepper
1 cup low-fat mayonnaise (see
  recipe on page 149)
1 tablespoon finely grated
  parmesan cheese

Cook potatoes in their skins until just tender. Peel
potatoes and chop roughly. Combine with onion,
capsicum, celery and carrot. Add pepper to taste, then add
mayonnaise and cheese. Spoon into a shallow, lightly oiled
ovenproof dish and bake at 180°C for 20 minutes or until
top begins to brown.

Potato salad with mint Serves 4–6

500 g washed new potatoes
$^1/_2$ cup finely chopped fresh mint
black pepper

1 cup low-fat mayonnaise (see
  recipe on page 149)

Cook potatoes in their skins until just tender. Cut
each potato into quarters and place in a serving bowl.
Add mint, pepper and mayonnaise. Toss well and chill
before serving.

Sesame greens
Serves 4–6

200 g topped and tailed green
  beans
100 g zucchini
100 g asparagus spears
200 g topped and tailed sugar
  peas

2 tablespoons low-salt soy sauce
1 tablespoon toasted sesame
  seeds

Cut beans, zucchini and asparagus spears into 5-cm
lengths. Cook all vegetables in boiling water until just
tender. Run under cold water and drain well. Combine
soy sauce and sesame seeds and toss through vegetables.
Let stand for at least 30 minutes before serving.

Tabouleh
Serves 4

$1/4$ cup burghul
2 tomatoes, peeled, seeded and
  finely chopped
3 spring onions, finely chopped
$1/2$ cup chopped fresh parsley

$1/2$ cup finely chopped fresh
  coriander
2 tablespoons tangy yoghurt
  dressing (see recipe on page 144)

Soak burghul in lukewarm water for 10 minutes. Drain
well. Combine all ingredients in a bowl and mix gently.
Be careful not to make a mush. Add dressing.

Tomato
moulds with dill sauce Serves 6

1 tablespoon gelatine
$^1/_4$ cup boiling water
1 cup salt-free tomato juice
$1^1/_4$ cups salt-free vegetable juice
2 cups cottage cheese or tofu

squeeze of fresh lemon
selection of mixed salad greens
  (for garnish)
1 quantity mustard and dill sauce
  (see recipe on page 149)

Dissolve gelatine in boiling water. Combine tomato juice, vegetable juice, cottage cheese or tofu and lemon juice, and purée until smooth. Add the gelatine mixture. Pour mixture into 6 moulds and refrigerate until firm. To serve, turn out onto individual plates garnished with salad greens and spoon dill sauce over the top.

Waldorf
salad Serves 4–6

2 red apples, cored and diced
2 Granny Smith apples, cored and
  diced
1 cup chopped celery

$^1/_4$ lettuce, roughly chopped
1 cup chopped walnuts
1 quantity tangy yoghurt dressing
  (see recipe on page 144)

Combine all ingredients and toss well.

Vegetables

Baby beets in orange sauce Serves 4-6

1 cup fresh orange juice
2 tablespoons tarragon vinegar
2 tablespoons long fine strips of
  orange rind

1 tablespoon cornflour
$^{1}/_{4}$ cup white wine
4 beetroot, cooked and peeled

Place orange juice, vinegar and orange rind in a saucepan
and bring to the boil. Blend cornflour in white wine
and add to orange liquid. Simmer gently until thickened.
Using a melon-baller, scoop beetroot into small balls.
Add beetroot to orange sauce. Heat through and serve
immediately.

Baked pumpkin with sesame seeds Serves 4-6

600–800 g pumpkin
1 cup low-fat yoghurt

sprinkle of sesame seeds

Peel and cut pumpkin into serving pieces. Cook pumpkin
in a little water until just tender, then brush the top of
each piece with low-fat yoghurt. Sprinkle with sesame
seeds. Place pumpkin pieces on a lightly oiled non-stick
baking tray and bake at 180°C until pumpkin is tender
and sesame seeds are golden.

Baked tomatoes   Serves 4

2 large ripe tomatoes
1 cup wholemeal breadcrumbs
1 onion, finely diced
$^1/_2$ teaspoon mixed herbs

2 tablespoons seeded and finely
  chopped green capsicum
$^1/_4$ cup grated low-fat grating
  cheese

Cut tomatoes in half and remove seeds. Combine remaining ingredients. Spoon mixture into tomatoes and bake at 180°C for 20 minutes or until tomatoes are tender and filling begins to brown.

Cabbage casserole   Serves 4–6

4–6 cabbage leaves, blanched
2 large onions, sliced
$^1/_2$ kg shredded cabbage (red or
  white)
2 large apples, cored, peeled and
  sliced

4 large potatoes, peeled,
  parboiled and sliced
250 g cottage cheese or tofu
black pepper
2 tablespoons parmesan cheese
sprinkle of cinnamon

Line a lightly oiled ovenproof dish with blanched cabbage leaves. Place a layer of onion and then cabbage, apple and potato. Cover with cottage cheese or tofu and sprinkle with pepper. Repeat layers, finishing with a layer of potato, and top with parmesan cheese. Sprinkle with cinnamon and cover with foil. Bake at 170°C for 40 minutes. Remove foil and bake a further 10 minutes until potatoes are lightly browned.

Note This is excellent as a meal on its own with hot bread rolls and a salad of your choice.

Cauliflower
in sesame sauce Serves 6-8

1 cauliflower, broken into pieces
1 quantity white sauce (see recipe
  on page 152)

¼ cup sesame seeds

Lightly steam cauliflower. Heat white sauce. Toast sesame seeds under griller. Place cauliflower pieces on a serving dish. Cover with white sauce and sprinkle with sesame seeds. Bake at 180°C for 10 minutes to brown.

Note You can substitute ½ cup raw coconut for sesame seeds. Toast under griller and add to sauce. This is a great vegetable dish to serve with a fish, chicken or meat curry.

Corn
and potato bake Serves 4

2 cups wholemeal breadcrumbs
4 large potatoes, peeled,
  parboiled and sliced
2 cups ricotta cheese

black pepper
4 cups cooked corn kernels
½ cup grated low-fat grating
  cheese

Spread 1 cup breadcrumbs over the base of a lightly oiled ovenproof dish. Top with a layer of potato. Combine ricotta cheese, pepper and corn and mix well. Spread a small amount of corn mixture over potato. Follow with a layer of potato. Repeat until all potatoes and corn mixture are used. Combine grated cheese and remaining breadcrumbs and spread over the top of casserole. Bake at 180°C for 20–30 minutes or until golden brown.

Corn fritters   Serves 6

2 cups cooked corn kernels
1 onion, finely diced
3 egg whites
$^1/_4$ cup low-fat milk
1 cup unbleached wholemeal plain
  flour

$^1/_2$ teaspoon paprika
1 teaspoon baking powder
black pepper

Combine all ingredients. Drop spoonfuls onto a lightly oiled non-stick pan and cook for 3 minutes. Turn to brown other side. Serve with salad.

Creamy mashed potatoes   Serves 4-6

600–800 g peeled and chopped
  potatoes
$^1/_2$–1 cup low-fat milk

black pepper
$^1/_4$ cup chopped fresh parsley or
  chives

Place potatoes in a saucepan, cover with water and cook until tender. Drain well. Add enough low-fat milk to purée potatoes to a smooth consistency. Add pepper and parsley or chives to taste.

Note Finely chopped walnuts, sesame seeds or cashew nuts make an interesting nutty variation to this basic recipe.

Ginger garlic beans Serves 4

½ kg topped and tailed green
  beans
1 clove garlic, crushed

3-cm piece fresh ginger, peeled,
  sliced and finely chopped
¼ cup water

Lightly oil a non-stick wok or frying pan. Add beans,
garlic and ginger. Toss quickly. Add water, cover and
cook for just a few minutes or until beans are tender.
Serve immediately.

Green beans with bean shoots Serves 4

⅓ cup chicken stock (see recipe
  on page 40)
1 teaspoon finely chopped fresh
  dill
2 cups celery, diagonally cut into
  3-cm pieces

1½ cups green beans, cut into
  3-cm lengths
black pepper
500 g bean shoots

Heat a wok or small non-stick frying pan. Add chicken
stock. As it bubbles furiously, add all ingredients except
bean shoots. Keep ingredients moving while they cook for
2 minutes. Add bean shoots and cook a further 1 minute.
Serve immediately.

Honey and clove beetroot Serves 4

4 medium beetroot, washed
  thoroughly
1 tablespoon honey

1 tablespoon cider vinegar
6 cloves

Cover beetroot with water and simmer until tender. Peel quickly while beetroot are still hot. Add honey, vinegar and cloves and cover.

Note This beetroot is excellent served with cold lean meats or in sandwiches.

Leek casserole Serves 4

6 leeks, washed and chopped
2 cups celery, cut into 3-cm
  chunks
2 cups carrot, cut into chunks
2 cups potato, peeled and cut into
  chunks

$1^1/_2$ litres chicken stock (see
  recipe on page 40)
1 x 425 g can salt-free tomato
  pieces in juice
black pepper or 4 peppercorns
$^1/_2$ cup chopped fresh parsley

Add leeks, celery, carrot and potato to the chicken stock. Simmer until vegetables are tender. Place vegetables and cooking liquid in a casserole dish. Add tomatoes, pepper or peppercorns and parsley. Cover and cook at 180°C for 30 minutes.

Note This dish may be thickened with a cornflour mixture (1 tablespoon cornflour mixed to a paste with 2 tablespoons cold water).

Lemon mint carrots Serves 4-6

½ kg carrots
150 ml chicken stock (see recipe
  on page 40)

1 tablespoon chopped fresh mint
juice of ½ lemon

Cut carrots into julienne strips and steam lightly in chicken stock. Drain. Squeeze over lemon juice and sprinkle with mint. Let stand for 5 minutes before serving.

Parsnip fritters Serves 4

12 pieces parsnip, peeled and
  sliced into thin rings

BATTER
125 g unbleached wholemeal plain
  flour
2 egg whites
200 ml low-fat milk
black pepper

Lightly steam parsnip rings until tender. Drain well and dry on paper towels.

To make the batter, combine all batter ingredients and let stand for 15–30 minutes. Dip parsnip pieces into mixture. Cook fritters in a lightly oiled non-stick pan until both sides are golden brown.

Pumpkin au gratin Serves 4

500 g peeled and sliced pumpkin
black pepper
1/4 teaspoon nutmeg
1/4 teaspoon ground cloves
3 egg whites

1/4 cup low-fat milk
1/4 cup low-fat yoghurt
1/2 cup grated low-fat grating
  cheese

Cook pumpkin in a little water until tender, and drain. Combine with pepper, a dash of nutmeg and cloves. Place in an ovenproof casserole dish. Beat egg whites, milk, yoghurt and half of the grated cheese. Pour over pumpkin. Sprinkle with remaining cheese. Bake at 180°C for 15–20 minutes or until top is brown.

Pumpkin fritters Serves 4

8 slices pumpkin, cut 2-cm thick

BATTER
1 cup unbleached wholemeal plain
  flour
1 teaspoon curry powder

1 teaspoon paprika
1 cup low-fat milk
2 egg whites
wholemeal breadcrumbs and
  sesame seeds

Cook pumpkin slices until tender but not too soft. Drain on paper towels and cool.

To make the batter, combine all batter ingredients – except breadcrumbs and sesame seeds. Dip pumpkin slices into batter and then press into breadcrumb and sesame seed mixture. Cook on a lightly oiled non-stick pan until coating is golden brown. Turn and repeat on other side.

Savoury pikelets   Makes 12

1 cup unbleached white self-raising flour
½ teaspoon curry powder
¼ teaspoon cumin powder
½ teaspoon mustard powder

1 cup low-fat milk or low-fat soymilk
2 whole eggs or 3 egg whites
2 tablespoons grated low-fat grating cheese

Blend all ingredients – except cheese. Add cheese and fold through. Let stand for 30 minutes before cooking. Drop spoonfuls of mixture onto a lightly oiled non-stick pan. Cook until mixture bubbles. Turn and cook to brown other side. Serve warm with cottage cheese and top with tomato slices, mashed cooked asparagus, cooked well-drained spinach, cooked corn kernels, chopped black or green olives, diced red and green capsicum or grated carrot.

Sherry turnips in yoghurt   Serves 4–6

½ kg peeled turnips
1 tablespoon dry sherry
2 cups low-fat yoghurt

1 tablespoon finely chopped fresh dill
black pepper

Cut turnips into strips and place in a saucepan. Cover with water and simmer until tender. Drain well. Add sherry and let stand for 20 minutes. Add yoghurt, dill and pepper. Reheat but do not boil. Serve as a vegetable accompaniment with cold or hot lean meats.

Spinach buns Serves 6

6 wholemeal rolls
$1/2$ kg cooked, drained and finely
  shredded spinach
2 cups cottage cheese or tofu

3 egg whites
black pepper
$1/4$ teaspoon nutmeg

Remove tops from buns. Scoop out bread and make into breadcrumbs. Combine breadcrumbs with remaining ingredients. Spoon mixture evenly into buns and replace tops. Wrap in foil and bake at 180°C for 30 minutes. Serve with salad.

Stuffed beetroot Serves 4

4 medium beetroot, washed and
  peeled
2 tablespoons grated apple
2 tablespoons grated onion
2 tablespoons chopped capsicum
  (red or green)

$1/2$ cup wholemeal breadcrumbs
squeeze of fresh lemon
black pepper

Cut the tops away and make a hollow through the centre of each beetroot using an apple corer. Mix remaining ingredients and fill in the hollows. Wrap each beetroot in foil and place in a water bath. Bake at 180°C for 1 hour or until beetroot are tender.

Stuffed
jacket potatoes Serves 4

4 potatoes   filling (see below)

Bake potatoes in their jackets at 180°C until tender when
pierced with a skewer. Slice the tops off the potatoes and
scoop out the filling, but leave a firm casing. Be careful
not to pierce the skin. Fill the potatoes with your choice
of filling and return to the oven. Add a topping such as
parmesan or low-fat grating cheese, wholemeal
breadcrumbs, chopped fresh herbs, or even a mixture of
wholemeal breadcrumbs, tomato paste and chopped fresh
herbs, and bake at 180°C for 10–15 minutes or until tops
are golden brown.

FILLINGS
Apple filling
Combine flesh from 4 potatoes; ¼ cup finely grated
low-fat cheese; 1 small apple, peeled and grated; and
1–2 teaspoons Dijon mustard.

Celery and walnut filling
Combine flesh from 4 potatoes; 30 g ricotta cheese;
4 tablespoons finely chopped celery; 2 tablespoons finely
chopped walnuts; and black pepper to taste.

Ricotta cheese and chives filling
Combine flesh from 4 potatoes; 30 g ricotta cheese;
2 teaspoons finely chopped fresh chives; black pepper to
taste; and 1 egg white.

Shrimp filling
Combine flesh from 4 potatoes; 30 g shelled shrimps;
4 spring onions, finely chopped; ½ teaspoon lemon rind;
½ teaspoon chopped fresh parsley; ¼ teaspoon cayenne
pepper; and 1 egg white.

Tomato cheese filling

Combine flesh from 4 potatoes; 2 tablespoons salt-free tomato paste; 1 teaspoon dry basil; ¼ teaspoon black pepper; 1 tomato, peeled, seeded and chopped; and 1 egg white. Fill baked potato and sprinkle with finely grated low-fat grating cheese.

Stuffed onions Serves 6

6 large onions
1 cup wholemeal breadcrumbs
1 Granny Smith apple, grated
1 cup finely chopped celery
¼ cup finely chopped almonds

pinch allspice
1 egg white
juice of 1 small lemon
½ cup grated low-fat grating cheese

Peel onions and cut in half crosswise. Carefully remove the centres. Chop the centres very finely and add to breadcrumbs, apple, celery, almonds, allspice and egg white. Fill onions with this mixture.

Place onions in a lightly oiled non-stick baking dish. Add lemon juice. Cover and bake at 180°C for 15–20 minutes. Remove and sprinkle with grated cheese. Return onions to oven uncovered and bake for a further 5 minutes or until cheese has melted and browned. Serve on a bed of rice.

Sweet and sour cabbage Serves 6

$^1/_2$ cup raisins soaked for 30
  minutes in $^1/_2$ cup fresh orange
  juice
4 cups shredded cabbage
3 onions, sliced
4 apples, cored and chopped
$^1/_2$ cup apple cider

SAUCE
1 teaspoon cornflour
200 ml salt-free vegetable juice
$^1/_2$ cup unsweetened pineapple
  juice
200 g salt-free tomato pieces,
  drained
2 tablespoons wine vinegar
black pepper

Drain raisins and add to cabbage, onions, apples and apple
cider. Simmer with lid on for 5 minutes.

To make the sauce, combine cornflour with a little
vegetable juice to make a paste and stir into remaining
sauce ingredients. Add this to the cabbage. Cook a further
5 minutes.

Sweet cinnamon beetroot Serves 4

8 baby beetroot, washed and
  peeled
1 cup fresh orange juice

2 tablespoons finely grated orange
  rind
1–2 teaspoons cinnamon

Place beetroot in a saucepan. Add orange juice, orange
rind and cinnamon. Gently simmer for 1 hour or until
beetroot are tender. Add more water if necessary during
the cooking. Serve immediately.

Turnips in lemon sauce Serves 4–6

500 g peeled and sliced small
   turnips
1 cup fresh orange juice
2 tablespoons finely grated orange
   or lemon rind

1 cup water
1 tablespoon Dijon mustard
fresh lemon juice
1 tablespoon finely chopped fresh
   parsley

Cook turnips in orange juice, rind and water for 10–15 minutes or until tender. Drain and cover so that they steam themselves dry. Keep ½ cup of cooking liquid. Blend in mustard and lemon juice, and stir in turnips. Heat through and sprinkle with parsley before serving.

Vegetable casserole with orange swede sauce
Serves 6–8

4 large potatoes, peeled and
   chopped
2 carrots, chopped
1 parsnip, peeled and chopped
1 cup celery chunks
1 cup green peas
1 cup chopped green beans
2 x 425 g cans salt-free tomato
   pieces, drained
1 green capsicum, seeded and cut
   into chunks

1 red capsicum, seeded and cut
   into chunks
2 cups fresh orange juice
1 tablespoon finely grated orange
   rind
2 cups water or chicken or
   vegetable stock (see recipes on
   pages 40 and 45)
2 cups grated swede
black pepper

Place all ingredients in a large earthenware casserole dish. Bake at 170°C, with lid on, for 2 hours. Dish is ready to eat when vegetables are tender and liquid has reduced to a thick sauce. Serve with rice, pasta or couscous.

Zucchini boats   Serves 4

8 long zucchini (approximately
15–20 cm)
1 onion, finely diced
1 clove garlic, crushed
2 tomatoes, peeled, seeded and
chopped

1 small red capsicum, seeded and
finely diced
1 teaspoon chopped capers
$^1/_2$ teaspoon basil
$^1/_2$ teaspoon finely grated orange
rind

Blanch zucchini in boiling water for 6 minutes. Drain. Halve carefully and scoop out seeds. Discard seeds. Place in a flat ovenproof casserole dish.

Combine remaining ingredients in a saucepan. Stir over low heat until mixture boils. Boil for 1 minute. Remove from heat and spoon mixture into zucchini halves. Bake at 180°C for 15–20 minutes. Add a topping such as parmesan or low-fat grating cheese, wholemeal breadcrumbs, chopped fresh herbs, or even a mixture of wholemeal breadcrumbs, tomato paste and chopped fresh herbs.

Zucchini omelette   Serves 1

3 egg whites
1 small zucchini, grated
2 tablespoons finely chopped
fresh parsley

2 tablespoons finely chopped
fresh chives
black pepper

Lightly beat egg whites. Add remaining ingredients and pour into a lightly oiled non-stick omelette pan. When mixture is firm, turn over and cook other side. Serve on wholemeal toast or roll up and serve with salad.

Main
meals

Caraway
and pumpkin pasties Makes 6

1 quantity wholemeal potato
  pastry (see recipe on page 132)
1 cup grated pumpkin
1 Granny Smith apple, grated
1 small onion, finely diced
$^1/_2$ cup finely chopped celery

$^1/_2$ cup finely shredded cabbage
black pepper
1 teaspoon caraway seeds
1 egg white
extra egg white, beaten

Cut pastry into squares or circles. Combine remaining ingredients – except extra egg white – and mix well. Spoon mixture on one side of pastry square or circle and fold over. Press edges together. Wipe tops of pasties with extra egg white and sprinkle liberally with caraway seeds. Bake at 180°C for 15 minutes, then lower heat to 170°C and cook a further 10–15 minutes.

Carrot
and onion loaf Serves 4

6 cups cooked mashed carrots
1 cup wholemeal breadcrumbs
5 egg whites
$^1/_2$ cup low-fat milk

$^1/_4$ teaspoon cayenne pepper
4 onions, chopped
2 tablespoons chopped fresh
  chives or parsley

Combine carrots and breadcrumbs. Mix well. Add remaining ingredients and mix well. Press into a loaf tin. Cover with foil and place in a water bath. Bake at 180°C for 40 minutes or until firm.

Chicken
and carrot loaf Serves 6–8

500–750 g minced raw chicken (no
  skin)
1 cup chopped fresh parsley
2$\frac{1}{4}$ cups grated carrot (3–4
  carrots)
1 small onion, diced

$\frac{1}{2}$ cup fine wholemeal
  breadcrumbs
black pepper
1$\frac{1}{4}$ cups low-fat yoghurt with a
  squeeze of fresh lemon

Combine chicken, ½ cup of parsley, 1½ cups carrot, onion, breadcrumbs, pepper and yoghurt in a large bowl and mix well. Press a third of the mixture into a lined or lightly oiled 23 x 13 x 8-cm glass terrine. Sprinkle the remaining carrot over the top and press down firmly. Add another third of the chicken mixture, pressing down well, and sprinkle over remaining parsley. Top with chicken mixture and press down firmly.

Cover with foil and place in a water bath. Bake at 170°C for 40 minutes. Leave to cool in glass terrine. Gently ease a metal spatula around the sides of the chicken loaf, turn onto a plate and chill well before serving. Serve with salad and fresh wholemeal rolls.

Note This is an excellent loaf for a picnic lunch.

Chicken
breast in filo pastry Serves 6

2 cups grated Granny Smith apple
$^1/_2$ cup roughly chopped walnuts
  or almonds
$^1/_2$ cup low-fat yoghurt
2 tablespoons date and apple
  chutney (see recipe on page 155)

$^1/_2$ cup sultanas or raisins
black pepper
6 chicken fillets (no skin),
  flattened
1 x 200 g packet filo pastry
extra low-fat yoghurt

Combine apple, walnuts or almonds, yoghurt, chutney, sultanas or raisins and pepper. Spread this fruit mixture over the flattened chicken fillets and fold up into a neat parcel.

Brush 2 sheets of filo pastry with extra yoghurt. Fold in half and brush once more. Place the chicken on the end of the pastry sheet nearest to you. Fold the sides of the pastry sheet up over the chicken to form a parcel. Continue with remaining chicken and filo. Place chicken parcels on a lined baking tray with seam side down and bake at 180–200°C until pastry is golden brown and chicken is tender.

Note These parcels can be prepared ahead and kept in the refrigerator covered with plastic wrap.

Chicken
chow mein Serves 8

STOCK

2 teaspoons curry powder

2 cups chicken stock (see recipe on page 40)

2 teaspoons peeled and grated fresh ginger

2 onions, roughly chopped

3 tablespoons brown rice

1 cup chopped celery

1 cup chopped green beans

1 cup chopped green capsicum

1 cup shredded cabbage

2 cups cauliflower florets

500 g cooked chicken pieces (no skin)

Bring stock to the boil. Reduce heat and add remaining ingredients – except chicken. Simmer, covered, for 20 minutes. Add chicken and heat through. If necessary, this could be thickened with 1 teaspoon cornflour mixed with ¼ cup extra chicken stock. Serve on a bed of rice with large chunks of fresh pineapple.

Note You can substitute 500 g minced lean beef for chicken. Add meat to stock and cook gently for 10 minutes before adding vegetables.

Chinese whole fish

Serves 4–6

GARNISH
1 carrot, peeled and cut into
  julienne strips
2–3 spring onions, finely
  diagonally sliced
$1/2$ cup wine vinegar
$1/4$ cup fresh orange juice

1.5 kg whole fish (snapper,
  nannygai, trevally, terakihi)
$1/4$ cup fresh lemon juice
4–6 cups chicken stock (see recipe
  on page 40)
1 mild onion, diced
1 stick celery, diced
1 carrot, peeled and cut into
  julienne strips
1-cm piece fresh ginger, peeled
  and finely chopped
2 cloves garlic, crushed

Combine garnish ingredients and marinate for 1 hour.
Clean and scale fish. Rub the fish inside and out with
lemon juice. Place stock in a wok or large deep frying
pan. Add vegetables, ginger and garlic. Arrange a rack on
the base of the wok or frying pan. Bring stock to the boil
and place the fish on the rack. Cover and steam for 15–20
minutes or until cooked. (Alternatively, place fish in foil
and bake at 180°C for 30 minutes. Pour 1 cup of stock
and flavourings over the top.)

Place fish on heated serving dish. Bring the remaining
stock to a rapid boil and reduce by half. Spoon liquid over
fish. Drain carrots and spring onions, and sprinkle them
over fish to garnish. Serve immediately.

Note This dish may also be served cold.

Curried hot rice salad Serves 4–6

2 cups cooked brown rice
1 onion, chopped
1 red capsicum, seeded and
 chopped
1 green capsicum, seeded and
 chopped

1 cup grated carrot
1 cup chopped celery
2 teaspoons peeled and grated
 fresh ginger
2 teaspoons curry powder
black pepper

Combine all ingredients in a lightly oiled non-stick wok. Keep ingredients moving so they do not stick to base of wok. Cover and cook for 4–5 minutes. Serve immediately.

Fish and asparagus Serves 4

4 x 125 g fish steaks or cutlets or
 large fillets
1 x 310 g can cut asparagus spears
1/3 cup dry white wine
black pepper

small sprig of fresh rosemary
4 shallots, finely chopped
1 tablespoon unbleached
 wholemeal plain flour
3 tablespoons low-fat yoghurt

Arrange fish in a lightly oiled non-stick shallow ovenproof dish. Drain liquid from asparagus and set liquid aside. Scatter asparagus over fish, then pour wine over the top. Add pepper and rosemary. Cover with foil and bake at 180°C for about 25 minutes or until fish is tender. While fish is cooking, cook shallots in a little asparagus liquid. Combine flour and some asparagus liquid to make a paste. Stir this and remaining liquid in with shallots until sauce thickens. Arrange fish on a heated serving platter, pour liquid from fish into the sauce and stir in yoghurt. Gently reheat but do not boil. Pour sauce over fish and serve.

Fish
and chips   Serves 4

juice of 1 lemon
4 x 125 g fillets of fish (whiting,
  sea perch, ling)
1/2 cup unbleached wholemeal
  plain flour
1 teaspoon basil or parsley or
  chives

2 egg whites, lightly beaten
1 1/2 cups wholemeal breadcrumbs
4 large potatoes, peeled and cut
  into large chips
1/2 cup low-fat yoghurt

Squeeze lemon juice over fish. Dip fish in combined flour
and herbs and shake off excess. Dip in egg white and press
down in breadcrumbs until both sides are evenly coated.
Shake off any excess. Refrigerate crumbed fish for at least
2 hours prior to cooking. Cook fish in a lightly oiled
non-stick pan until both sides are golden brown. Do
not overcook.

Cook potatoes in water until tender but still firm. Toss
warm cooked chips with yoghurt in a bowl. Place chips on
a lightly oiled baking tray or a baking tray lined with non-
stick baking paper, and bake at 220°C for 10 minutes or
until potatoes are brown and crunchy. Serve immediately.

Fish
in mango sauce Serves 4

8 x 65 g fillets of whiting
1 cup chicken stock (see recipe on
  page 40)
black pepper
squeeze of fresh lemon

SAUCE
1 cup dry white wine
$^1/_2$ cup low-fat yoghurt
1 mango, peeled and sliced
black pepper

Poach fillets in chicken stock, pepper and lemon juice for about 3 minutes either side. Remove carefully to a heated platter and keep warm.

To make the sauce, use the same pan in which the fish has been poached. Pour out any leftover stock. Pour in white wine and yoghurt and keep heat on high for liquid to reduce. Add mango as the sauce reduces. (The mango takes only a couple of minutes to cook, so stir occasionally to avoid sticking.) The sauce takes approximately 4 minutes to cook and will turn a golden brown colour. Place the fish fillets on serving plates and spoon a small amount of sauce over them. Serve with salad greens.

Hot curried vegetables

Serves 4

2 cups chicken stock (see recipe
 on page 40)
1 clove garlic, crushed
1 teaspoon turmeric
$^3/_4$ teaspoon chilli powder
$^1/_2$ teaspoon ground ginger or
 1 teaspoon peeled and grated
 fresh ginger
1 teaspoon ground coriander
100 g carrot, cut into julienne strips
100 g zucchini, cut into julienne
 strips

50 g diagonally sliced celery
10 green beans, cut into 3-cm
 lengths
100 g cauliflower rosettes
200 g red and green capsicum,
 seeded and cut into strips
50 g peeled and sliced mushrooms
1 x 425 g can salt-free whole
 tomatoes and juice
$^1/_2$ cup chopped spring onions

Bring stock and spices to the boil. Add vegetables – except
tomatoes and spring onions – and simmer until just
tender. Add tomatoes and spring onions and heat through.
Serve with rice or noodles, a tossed green salad, a bowl
of chilled apple slices and a bowl of low-fat yoghurt.

Note If you do not like very hot curries, use only half
the herb and spice measurements given. If you are using
fresh ginger you can still use a full teaspoon measure.

Jellied chicken Serves 6

1.5 kg whole chicken (no skin)
$1/2$ lemon
few slices onion
1 small carrot, roughly chopped
6 black peppercorns
sprigs of fresh parsley
1 bay leaf
$2^1/4$ cups stock from chicken

6 teaspoons gelatine
$1/2$ cup dry white wine
$1/2$ small cucumber, seeded and
  cut into pieces
1 cup sliced celery
1 medium red capsicum, seeded
  and cut into wedges

Place chicken in a saucepan with lemon, onion, carrot, peppercorns, parsley and bay leaf. Add enough water to cover. Cover and cook very gently until chicken is tender. Leave chicken in stock until cool enough to handle. Remove meat from bones and set aside.

Return bones to stock and bring to the boil. Cover and boil gently for about 25 minutes. Strain. Measure amount of stock required and refrigerate to let fat come to surface. Skim off fat. Heat $1/2$ cup of measured stock, sprinkle in gelatine, and stir until dissolved. Add wine to remaining stock, heat and stir in dissolved gelatine. Pour a little into a mould or bowl rinsed with cold water and chill until set.

Arrange chicken and vegetables in the mould or bowl. Carefully pour in the gelatine mixture and chill until firm. Remove from mould, set on a platter and serve.

Kokanda
(African spicy fish dish) Serves 8

DRESSING

$1/4$ teaspoon cumin

black pepper

1 green chilli, seeded and finely
  minced

1 clove garlic, crushed

1 cup low-fat yoghurt

500–750 g cooked and roughly
  chopped white fish fillets

4 tablespoons fresh lime juice

4 tablespoons fresh lemon juice

125 g freshly grated coconut

1 red capsicum, seeded and cut
  into thin strips

1 green capsicum, seeded and cut
  into thin strips

2 bananas, peeled and thinly
  diagonally sliced

4 medium tomatoes, peeled,
  seeded and chopped

1 cucumber, peeled, seeded and
  chopped

125 g chopped fresh pineapple

Shake all dressing ingredients in a jar and let stand for
4 hours to allow flavours to blend.

Mix fish, lime and lemon juice. Leave to marinate for
1 hour in a cool place. Turn fish frequently. Drain. Reserve
1 tablespoon of marinade and add to the dressing. Place
fish in a serving dish and add remaining ingredients. Toss
well. Pour dressing over the top and chill for an hour
before serving. Serve on a bed of crisp lettuce leaves.

Pancakes
with savoury chicken filling Serves 6–8

PANCAKE MIXTURE
1$^1/_2$ cups low-fat milk
$^1/_2$ cup low-fat yoghurt
2 egg whites
1 cup unbleached white plain flour
1 cup wholemeal plain flour
$^1/_2$ cup fresh orange juice

FILLING
500 g cold cooked chicken (no
  skin)
1 quantity tomato capsicum sauce
  (see recipe on page 151)
$^1/_4$ teaspoon allspice

TOPPING
1 cup white sauce (see recipe on
  page 152)
$^1/_4$ cup grated low-fat grating
  cheese

To make the pancakes, combine all pancake ingredients and blend to make a smooth batter. Let mixture stand for 30 minutes before cooking. Heat a lightly oiled non–stick pan. Pour in enough batter to cover base of pan. When bubbles appear, turn pancake and cook other side for just a few seconds to brown lightly. Remove and continue this procedure until all mixture has been used. Keep pancakes warm as you cook all the mixture.

To make the filling, add chicken to tomato capsicum sauce and season with allspice. Spread filling in each pancake and then roll pancakes into tubes. Place pancakes next to each other in a rectangular baking dish. Pour white sauce over the top and sprinkle with cheese. Bake at 180°C until well heated and cheese is golden brown.

Pizza for all the family

BASE
wholemeal pita breads

SAUCE
1 onion, diced
1 clove garlic, crushed
2 carrots, grated
1 x 425 g can salt-free tomatoes
  and juice

2 tablespoons salt-free tomato
  paste
$^1/_2$ cup water or stock or white
  wine
1 teaspoon basil
black pepper

Arrange pita breads on a pizza tray.

To make the sauce, purée all sauce ingredients. Place in a saucepan. Bring to the boil and allow to simmer for 10–20 minutes or until sauce begins to thicken. Cool before using.

Spoon some sauce over pita breads. Add toppings of your choice. Bake at 200°C for 5–10 minutes.

TOPPINGS

Capsicum
Red, green or yellow, seeded and sliced into strips or rings; quartered, precooked and chargrilled.

Cheese
Ricotta cheese (use firm for slicing); cottage cheese; tofu (use firm for slicing); goat's cheese; light mozzarella; fresh parmesan finely grated or thinly sliced.

Mushrooms
Mushrooms, thinly sliced; mushrooms marinated in low-salt soy sauce; precooked chargrilled mushrooms; precooked, drained forest mushrooms.

OPPOSITE:
*Strawberries in
brandy and
orange syrup
(see page 116).*

Onions

Spanish onions, thinly sliced; precooked chargrilled Spanish onion wedges; spring onions, diagonally sliced; white onions, diced; precooked and chargrilled leeks (long pieces).

Tomatoes

Roma tomatoes, thinly sliced; precooked roma tomato halves; cherry tomato halves; yellow pear tomato halves.

Zucchini

Green or yellow, thinly sliced into rounds; precooked and chargrilled, thinly sliced.

Extras

- Canned and well-drained artichoke hearts
- Canned or precooked and well-drained asparagus spears
- Cooked and chopped chicken meat (no skin)
- Seeded and chopped chillies
- Precooked and chargrilled eggplant
- Dry roasted garlic cloves
- Chopped fresh herbs (basil, parsley, chives, oregano, rosemary, coriander)
- Black or green olives
- Unsweetened crushed pineapple
- Pine nuts, sesame seeds and pumpkin kernels
- Cooked and chopped prawns
- Precooked and chargrilled pumpkin, thinly sliced
- Cold, cooked salmon or tuna, broken up
- Precooked and well-drained spinach

OPPOSITE: *Filled apple cake (see page 124).*

Potato flan Serves 6

1 quantity wheatgerm pastry (see recipe on page 131)

FILLING
2 medium potatoes, peeled and grated
4 egg whites
1/4 cup low-fat milk
2 tablespoons grated low-fat grating cheese

2 tablespoons cold chopped chicken (no skin)
1 tablespoon chopped fresh parsley
1 tablespoon chopped fresh chives
1 onion, finely chopped
1 clove garlic, chopped

Press pastry into an ovenproof flan dish.

Squeeze moisture from potatoes and dry. Place egg whites in bowl and whisk in milk. Add potatoes and remaining ingredients. Pour into prepared pastry base and bake at 180°C for 45 minutes or until well set and browned on top.

Potato flapjacks   Serves 8

1/4 cup low-fat milk
1 cup wholemeal plain flour
3 egg whites, lightly beaten
1/2 cup chopped celery

1/2 cup chopped onion
1/2 cup rolled oats
2 kg potatoes, peeled and grated
black pepper

Add milk to flour and mix to a smooth batter. Add eggs
and stir well. Add celery, onion, rolled oats and potato.
Combine well. Season with pepper.

Heat a lightly oiled non–stick pan and drop spoonfuls of
mixture onto pan surface and flatten. Cook about 4
flapjacks at a time. Cook for 2 minutes or until golden
brown. Turn over and cook other side for 1 minute.
Repeat until all mixture has been used. Keep hot.

Place 2 flapjacks, one on top of the other, on a serving
plate, top with shredded lettuce, slices of tomato,
cucumber and alfalfa sprouts, or serve plain with
horseradish cream (see recipe on page 147).

Note This recipe should make 16 flapjacks.

Pumpkin
almond pie Serves 8

BASE

1 cup wheatgerm

1 cup wholemeal breadcrumbs

FILLING

500 g grated pumpkin

4 potatoes, peeled and grated

2 cups wholemeal breadcrumbs

1 onion, grated

1 cup finely chopped celery

$^1/_4$ teaspoon nutmeg

$^1/_4$ teaspoon cayenne pepper

4 egg whites

$^1/_2$ cup low-fat milk

TOPPING

$^1/_2$ cup bran

$^1/_2$ cup flaked almonds

Line a round 20-cm springform cake tin with non-stick baking paper. Combine wheatgerm and breadcrumbs. Press down well in the base of the cake tin. If mixture is too dry, add a little water so crumbs stick together.

To make the filling, combine all filling ingredients and mix well. Press mixture firmly over base. Mix bran and almonds and sprinkle them over the filling. Cover with foil and secure foil with string. Bake at 170°C for 50–60 minutes. Remove foil and cook a further 10 minutes until almonds brown slightly. Serve hot or cold, but if serving hot let pie stand for a few minutes. Serve with salad.

Raisin and walnut rice Serves 4-6

100 g brown rice
pinch turmeric
$^1/_2$ cup raisins
$^1/_4$ cup fresh lemon juice

50 g chopped walnuts
1 teaspoon cumin seed
$1^1/_2$ tablespoons shredded coconut

Cook rice in water with turmeric. Drain and cool. Soak raisins in lemon juice until most of the juice has been absorbed. Drain off excess liquid.

Combine all ingredients in a lightly oiled non-stick wok or frying pan. Keep ingredients moving so they do not stick to base of pan. Cover and cook for 4–5 minutes. Serve immediately.

Salmon potato casserole Serves 4

3 large potatoes, peeled and
  thinly sliced
1 x 220 g can salmon, drained
1 x 425 g can salt-free tomatoes
  and juice
1 cup chopped celery

1 cup seeded and chopped green
  capsicum
1 cup grated carrot
1 cup chopped fresh parsley
black pepper
breadcrumbs

Place a layer of potatoes, then flaked salmon on the base of a lightly oiled non-stick ovenproof dish. Cover with layers of tomato, celery, capsicum and carrot. Sprinkle with parsley and season with pepper. Repeat layers until all vegetables are used. Sprinkle breadcrumbs over the top and cook at 170°C for approximately 40 minutes or until breadcrumbs are golden brown. Serve with broccoli.

Soya bean patties Serves 4-6

500 g dried or canned soya beans
2 medium onions, chopped
1 tablespoon chopped fresh
  parsley
1 cup mashed potato
1 egg white
1 tablespoon salt-free tomato
  paste

black pepper
1 cup unbleached wholemeal plain
  flour
2 egg whites and 2 tablespoons
  low-fat milk, beaten
1 cup wholemeal breadcrumbs

Soak beans overnight. Discard water, then cover with fresh water and bring to the boil. Simmer until beans are tender. Drain and cool. If you are using canned beans, simply drain and rinse under cold water.

Drain and mash beans well. Combine with onions, parsley, potato, egg white, tomato paste and pepper. Form into patties, coat with flour, dip into egg white and milk mixture, and coat with breadcrumbs. Cook on a lightly oiled non-stick pan until golden brown on both sides and serve with a tossed green salad.

Spaghetti
and meatballs Serves 6

MEATBALLS

250 g lean ground beef
1 onion, finely minced
1 mashed banana
1 Granny Smith apple, peeled and
  finely grated
black pepper

TOMATO SAUCE

1 onion, diced
$1/2$ green capsicum, seeded and
  finely diced
1 stick celery, finely diced
1 x 425 g can salt-free tomatoes
  and juice, chopped

2 tablespoons salt-free tomato
  paste
1 clove garlic, crushed
$1/2$ teaspoon basil
$1/2$ teaspoon oregano
black pepper
chopped fresh parsley (for
  garnish)

500 g wholemeal spaghetti
3 litres boiling water

To make the meatballs, combine all meatball ingredients
and roll into very small balls. Place in a small frying pan in
3 cm of simmering water. Cook for 8 minutes, turning
once. Remove from pan and drain well. Keep hot.

To make the sauce, cook onion, capsicum and celery in 2
tablespoons water for 3 minutes. Add remaining
ingredients – except parsley – and cook for 40 minutes.

Cook spaghetti in boiling water until al dente. Drain.
Place spaghetti on serving plates, divide meatballs evenly
and pour sauce over the top. Garnish with parsley.

Spaghetti
and spinach sauce Serves 6

SAUCE
2 bunches spinach
2 cloves garlic
60 g pine nuts
2 tablespoons chopped fresh basil
  or 1 teaspoon basil
$1/4$ cup chopped fresh parsley
black pepper

500 g wholemeal spaghetti
3 litres boiling water

To make the sauce, cook spinach in a little water until it begins to wilt. Drain well. Combine remaining ingredients and purée until smooth.

Cook spaghetti in boiling water until al dente. Drain. Place spaghetti on serving plates and pour sauce over the top.

Note For a creamy texture add ½ cup cottage cheese or tofu.

Spaghetti
with tomato and mushroom sauce

Serves 6

SAUCE

1 large onion, diced

1 green capsicum, seeded and chopped

2 sticks celery, chopped

1 cup finely sliced mushrooms

1 cup grated carrot

1 x 425 g can salt-free tomatoes and juice

$1/4$ cup salt-free tomato paste

1 cup water or dry wine

2 cloves garlic

$1/2$–1 teaspoon basil

$1/2$–1 teaspoon oregano

2 bay leaves

black pepper

500 g wholemeal spaghetti

3 litres boiling water

To make the sauce, cook onion, capsicum, celery, mushrooms and carrot in $1/4$ cup water for 5 minutes. Add remaining ingredients and cook gently for 30–40 minutes.

Cook spaghetti in boiling water until al dente. Drain. Place spaghetti on serving plates and pour sauce over the top.

For a baked spaghetti dish, combine spaghetti and sauce in a lightly oiled non–stick ovenproof dish. Sprinkle a mixture of 1 cup fine wholemeal breadcrumbs and ½ cup grated low-fat grating cheese over the top and bake at 180°C for 30 minutes. Alternatively, serve spaghetti in a serving dish, with sauce on top.

Steamed
whole chicken <small>Serves 4–6</small>

1 medium chicken
¹/₂ lemon
¹/₄ cup fresh orange juice or apple
  juice or dry wine
1¹/₂ cups water

sprigs of fresh parsley
1 stick celery (with leaves)
¹/₂ carrot, chopped
black pepper

Completely remove all skin from chicken as well as any visible fat, then place chicken in a saucepan into which it fits neatly. Place lemon in chicken cavity and pour juice or wine and water over the top of chicken. Place parsley, celery and carrot in saucepan around chicken and season with pepper. Bring to the boil. Cover. Turn down heat to its lowest and simmer for 30 minutes. Test to see if chicken is cooked and remove from stock.

Pull chicken meat away from the carcass and discard bones. Cover meat so it does not dry out. The cooking liquid can be boiled, reduced by half and used as a stock for making soups and gravies, and for flavouring casseroles, stirfries and sauces.

Note To make a garlic chicken, wipe inside of chicken with 2 cloves of crushed garlic. Follow instructions for above but leave out last four ingredients.

Sweet and sour rice

Serves 6–8

¹/₄ cup unsweetened pineapple
  juice
1 teaspoon peeled and grated
  fresh ginger
1 onion, chopped
1 cup raisins
2 cups cold cooked brown rice
1 cup chopped celery
¹/₂ cup seeded and chopped red
  capsicum

¹/₂ cup seeded and chopped green
  capsicum
1 cup coarsely grated carrot
1 cup pineapple chunks
¹/₂ cup chopped fresh parsley
black pepper
¹/₄ teaspoon cumin
¹/₄ cup sesame seeds or sunflower
  seeds

In a cold wok, add pineapple juice, ginger, onion and raisins. Heat to boiling and add remaining ingredients. Keep mixture moving. Cover and cook for 5 minutes.

Tuna bake

Serves 4–6

1 x 425 g can tuna in water,
  drained
3 cups cooked wholemeal
  macaroni or cooked brown rice
1 x 440 g can unsweetened
  pineapple pieces, drained
1 cup cooked corn kernels
¹/₂ cup seeded and chopped red
  capsicum

¹/₂ cup seeded and chopped green
  capsicum
2 spring onions, chopped
black pepper
2 x quantities white sauce (see
  recipe on page 152)
1 cup wholemeal breadcrumbs
¹/₄ cup grated low-fat grating
  cheese

Combine first 8 ingredients in a lightly oiled ovenproof dish. Pour white sauce over the top, and sprinkle with breadcrumbs and cheese. Bake at 180°C for 30 minutes.

Tuna cakes Makes 12 cakes

4 large potatoes, peeled
1 x 250 g can tuna in water,
  drained
2 spring onions, finely chopped
2 carrots, grated
juice of ½ lemon

1 cup ricotta cheese or tofu
1 egg white
black pepper
2 egg whites
2 tablespoons water
1½ cups wholemeal breadcrumbs

Cook potatoes until tender. Drain and mash. Leave to cool. Add tuna, spring onions, carrots, lemon juice, ricotta cheese or tofu, egg white and pepper. Mix thoroughly.

Combine egg whites and water. Take spoonfuls of the potato mixture and roll in hands, then dip in egg white and water mixture and roll in breadcrumbs. Shape into round cakes approximately 7 cm in diameter. Place cakes in the refrigerator for 2 hours to chill and firm. (This should prevent cakes from losing the breadcrumb mixture in the cooking process.) Cook cakes in a lightly oiled non-stick frying pan for 4 minutes either side or until golden brown. Serve with asparagus spears or snow peas.

Vegetable
fried rice   Serves 5

2 egg whites
2 cups cooked cold brown rice
1 small green capsicum, seeded
  and finely chopped
1 medium onion, diced or 6 spring
  onions, chopped
125 g finely sliced mushrooms

1 medium carrot, grated
1 cup bean shoots
1 cup finely shredded cabbage
black pepper
$1/4$ teaspoon chilli powder
2 tablespoons finely chopped
  fresh parsley

Beat egg whites and cook on a lightly oiled non-stick pan. Turn and cook on both sides until firm. Remove from pan and chop roughly.

Heat a non-stick wok and lightly oil. Add all ingredients – except cooked egg white and parsley. Keep ingredients moving so they do not stick to base of pan. Cover and cook for 6–10 minutes. Add chopped egg and parsley. Serve immediately.

Vegetable
lasagne Serves 6–8

VEGETABLE SAUCE

1 medium onion, diced

2 cloves garlic, crushed

2 Granny Smith apples, peeled
and grated

2 medium carrots, grated

1 cup finely chopped celery

¹/₂ cup seeded and finely chopped
red capsicum

2 x 425 g cans salt-free tomatoes
and juice

¹/₂ cup salt-free tomato paste

1 cup water or stock or white
wine

1 teaspoon oregano

¹/₂ teaspoon basil

¹/₄ teaspoon ground rosemary

CHEESE SAUCE

125 g grated low-fat grating
cheese

1 quantity white sauce (see recipe
on page 152)

250 g instant lasagne noodles or
1 packet large wholemeal pita
breads, cut into lasagne noodle
shape

To make the vegetable sauce, place all sauce ingredients in
a saucepan. Bring to the boil. Turn down heat and simmer
for 40 minutes or until sauce has thickened slightly.

To make the cheese sauce, fold cheese into white sauce.

To make the lasagne, arrange layers of lasagne noodles or
pita bread shapes at the base of a lightly oiled rectangular
baking dish. Spread a layer of vegetable sauce and then a
layer of cheese sauce. Repeat layers, finishing with a layer
of cheese sauce. Bake at 180°C for 40 minutes. Serve
with salad.

Vegetable terrine Serves 6-8

4 large potatoes, peeled and
cubed
2–3 small carrots, chopped
3 zucchini, chopped
2 cups peas
2 sticks celery, chopped
1 red capsicum, seeded and
chopped
1 green capsicum, seeded and
chopped

2 tomatoes, peeled, seeded and
chopped
2 tablespoons finely chopped
fresh parsley
2 tablespoons finely chopped
fresh chives
5 teaspoons gelatine
$\frac{1}{2}$ cup chicken stock (see recipe
on page 40)
$\frac{1}{2}$ cup dry white wine

Cook potatoes until tender. Drain and cool. Combine
carrots, zucchini, peas, celery and capsicum and cook until
tender. Drain and cool. Combine potatoes, cooked
vegetables, tomato and herbs.

Combine gelatine with chicken stock. Dissolve over a low
heat. Add white wine. Leave to cool slightly. Wet the
inside of a glass terrine or mould. Pour a small amount of
the gelatine mixture to cover the base of the dish or
mould. Place this in the refrigerator to set slightly.

Arrange vegetables in dish or mould according to your
eye and pour in the remaining gelatine mixture. Place in
refrigerator for at least 2 hours or until required. Serve
with green salad and crusty wholemeal bread.

Zucchini
au gratin   Serves 8

2 cups uncooked brown rice
500–750 g diced zucchini
3 medium onions, diced
2 x 425 g cans salt-free tomatoes
  and juice, chopped
4 egg whites
2 cups low-fat milk
$\frac{1}{2}$ teaspoon thyme

$\frac{1}{4}$ teaspoon basil
$\frac{1}{2}$ teaspoon oregano
$\frac{1}{2}$ teaspoon nutmeg
black pepper
1 cup grated low-fat grating
  cheese
2 cups wholemeal breadcrumbs

Combine rice, zucchini, onions and tomatoes in a bowl. Combine juice from tomatoes, egg whites, milk, herbs and pepper in a separate bowl, and beat well. Add this mixture to the rice and vegetable mixture and pour into a lightly oiled non-stick ovenproof dish. Combine cheese and breadcrumbs and spread evenly over the dish. Bake at 180°C for 30–40 minutes.

Desserts

Apricot
and almond chews Makes 20

$^{1}/_{2}$ cup chopped dried apricots
$^{1}/_{4}$ cup fresh orange juice
2 tablespoons honey or apple
  juice concentrate
$^{1}/_{2}$ cup skim milk powder
$^{1}/_{4}$ cup roughly chopped almonds
1 tablespoon toasted sesame
  seeds

1 teaspoon finely grated orange
  rind
$^{1}/_{2}$ cup sultanas or currants
$^{1}/_{4}$ cup shredded coconut
extra shredded coconut

Place apricots, orange juice and honey or apple juice concentrate in a saucepan and simmer over low heat for 10 minutes or until apricots are tender. Do not drain. Mix in remaining ingredients – except extra coconut. Cool slightly.

Roll mixture into a log shape and then roll in extra coconut. Wrap in foil and keep in refrigerator. Cut into slices and store in a jar or wrap each individual piece in foil and cellophane.

Apricot
and cottage cheese pancakes Serves 4

PANCAKE MIXTURE
1 cup unbleached white self-
  raising flour
2 egg whites
2 tablespoons apple juice
  concentrate
1 cup low-fat milk or buttermilk

600 g stoned fresh apricots
1 cup fresh orange juice
1 tablespoon finely grated orange
  rind
$1/2$ teaspoon cinnamon
1 cup cottage cheese
$1/4$ cup toasted flaked almonds
extra fresh fruit (for garnish)

To make the pancakes, combine all pancake ingredients and blend to make a smooth batter. Let mixture stand for 30 minutes before cooking. Heat a lightly oiled non-stick pan. Pour in enough batter to cover base of pan. When bubbles appear, turn pancake and cook other side for just a few seconds to brown lightly. Remove and continue this procedure until all mixture has been used. Keep pancakes warm as you cook all the mixture.

Place apricots, orange juice, orange rind and cinnamon in a saucepan. Cover and cook apricots until just tender. Purée to make a smooth sauce.

To serve, place a pancake on an individual serving plate. Spoon ¼ cup cottage cheese on top and a spoonful of apricot sauce. Top with almonds. Garnish with sliced fresh apricot, peaches, banana, apple, pear or blackberries.

Note This recipe makes 8 small pancakes. Pancakes can be frozen.

105   Desserts

Banana freeze Serves 4–6

2 bananas, peeled and mashed
2 teaspoons fresh lemon juice
1/2 cup fresh orange juice
1 tablespoon finely grated orange
  or lemon rind
1/4 cup honey or apple juice
  concentrate
2 cups low-fat yoghurt
2 egg whites

Blend all ingredients – except egg whites – and pour into an ice-cream tray. Freeze until mixture starts to set. Remove from ice-cream tray and beat until smooth. Beat egg whites until stiff and fold through ice-cream mixture. Pour into clean, cold ice-cream trays and freeze. (Alternatively, combine ingredients, pour into an ice-cream maker and follow freezing instructions.) Serve with bananas and passionfruit pulp or wedges of mango and passionfruit or pineapple slices.

Banana pikelets Makes 12

1/2 cup unbleached white plain
  flour
1/2 cup unbleached wholemeal
  plain flour
1 teaspoon fresh lemon juice
1 teaspoon finely grated lemon
  rind
1 cup low-fat milk or low-fat
  soymilk
1 small banana, peeled and diced

Blend all ingredients – except banana. Add banana and fold through. Leave to stand for 30 minutes before cooking. Drop spoonfuls of mixture onto a lightly oiled non-stick pan. Cook until mixture bubbles. Turn and cook to brown other side. Serve warm with a squeeze of lemon juice and a light dusting of icing sugar.

Cassata

Serves 6-8

1 cup chopped almonds
1/2 cup chopped glacé cherries
1 cup mixed peel
1/2 cup chopped raisins

2 teaspoons brandy
1/4 cup toasted shredded coconut
1 litre low-fat ice-cream (see
  recipe on page 110)

Combine all ingredients – except ice-cream. Fold fruit and
nut mixture into ice-cream prior to freezing. Spoon into
parfait glasses and serve with fresh seasonal fruit.

Date and fig balls with apple slices

Makes approximately 30 balls

1 cup shredded coconut
1/2 cup finely chopped walnuts
1 cup chopped dates
250 g chopped dried figs
1 teaspoon fresh lemon juice

1/2 teaspoon finely grated lemon
  rind
extra finely chopped walnuts or
  sesame seeds

Blend coconut, walnuts, dates and figs in a food processor.
Add lemon juice and lemon rind. Knead mixture well.
Roll into small balls and coat with walnuts or sesame
seeds. Chill. Serve with a bowl of apple slices, bunches of
green grapes or chunks of pineapple.

Fruit pikelets   Makes 12

1 cup unbleached wholemeal flour
3 teaspoons baking powder
1 teaspoon cinnamon
1 cup low-fat milk or low-fat
  soymilk

2 whole eggs or 3 egg whites
$1/2$ cup finely chopped dried fruit
  (dates, apricots, sultanas,
  currants, figs, apples, mixed
  peel)

Blend all ingredients – except dried fruit. Add dried fruit and fold through. Stand for 30 minutes before cooking. Drop spoonfuls of mixture onto a lightly oiled non-stick pan. Cook until mixture bubbles. Turn and cook to brown other side. Serve lightly dusted with icing sugar.

Glazed kiwi fruit   Serves 4

3 tablespoons apricot fruit spread
  (see recipe on page 154)
2 tablespoons brandy

4 large kiwi fruit
2 large passionfruit

Place apricot spread and brandy in a small saucepan and heat through. Peel kiwi fruit and cut into slices. Overlap the slices on individual serving plates. Add passionfruit pulp to sauce, stir through and remove from heat. While still warm, spoon sauce evenly over kiwi fruit. Serve with low-fat ice-cream.

Lemon
cherry mould Serves 4

500 g stoned ripe cherries
3 teaspoons gelatine
2 tablespoons boiling water
grated rind of 1 lemon
2 tablespoons fresh lemon juice

1 tablespoon brandy
1 cup low-fat yoghurt
2 egg whites
extra cherries (for garnish)

Divide cherries equally between four dessert moulds. Dissolve gelatine in boiling water. Place lemon rind, lemon juice and brandy in a basin. Pour in gelatine. Mix in yoghurt and whisk. Whip egg whites until soft peaks form and fold through the yoghurt mixture. Pour over cherries.

Cover moulds with plastic wrap and put into the refrigerator to set. (This will take approximately 45 minutes.) Turn onto individual plates and decorate with fresh cherries.

Note You can substitute cherries with any fresh fruit.

Low-fat
vanilla ice-cream Makes 1 litre

1 x 375 ml evaporated low-fat milk
6 tablespoons skim milk powder
2 tablespoons honey or apple
  juice concentrate

1 tablespoon vanilla essence
4 egg whites

Combine first four ingredients and beat until thick and creamy. Place in the freezer for 40 minutes. Remove from freezer and rebeat for 3 minutes. Beat egg whites until fluffy and peaks form. Fold egg whites through milk mixture. Pour into ice-cream trays and freeze. (Alternatively, combine ingredients, pour into an ice-cream maker and follow freezing instructions.)

Orange
pineapple jelly Serves 6

3 teaspoons gelatine
1 cup boiling water
1 cup fresh orange juice

1 teaspoon finely grated lemon rind
1 cup unsweetened crushed
  pineapple

Dissolve gelatine in boiling water. Stir in orange juice and grated lemon rind. As jelly is nearly setting, fold through pineapple. Refrigerate until set. Serve with low-fat ice-cream or low-fat yoghurt.

Pawpaw
in passionfruit sauce   Serves 4

1 large pawpaw, peeled and
  seeded

$^1/_2$ cup fresh orange juice
3 large passionfruit

Cut pawpaw into chunky bite-sized pieces and place in a
serving bowl. Combine orange juice and passionfruit pulp
and pour over pawpaw. Marinate for 2–3 hours, tossing
often. Serve with low-fat ice-cream, low-fat yoghurt or
slices of crisp apple.

Peaches
with strawberry cream   Serves 4

1 punnet strawberries, hulled
1 tablespoon kirsch liqueur
  (optional)
$^1/_4$ cup low-fat yoghurt

4 large fresh ripe peaches
2 cups sliced hulled strawberries
  or raspberries

Purée strawberries, kirsch and yoghurt. Refrigerate.
Carefully skin peaches. (This can be done easily by placing
a skewer or fork into peach and holding over a gas flame
for approximately 1 or 2 minutes until skin bursts.) Cut
peaches in half, carefully scooping out the stone without
damaging the flesh. Place 2 peach halves on each serving
plate, fill with fresh strawberries or raspberries and pour
strawberry cream over the top.

Pears in passionfruit sauce Serves 4

1½ cups fresh orange juice
8 thin strips orange rind
4 well-ripened pears

¼ cup low-fat yoghurt
pulp of 2 passionfruit

Place orange juice and orange rind in saucepan and heat.
Peel pears and cut each into 8 pieces. Place pears into
liquid, turning pears occasionally, and simmer for 10
minutes or until pears are tender. Remove pears.

Add yoghurt and boil rapidly until juices thicken a
little. Remove from heat and add passionfruit pulp. Place
pears in a serving dish and spoon passionfruit sauce over
the top.

Pineapple and passionfruit mould Serves 8–10

1 x 440 g can crushed
  unsweetened pineapple, drained
pulp of 8 passionfruit
1 litre low-fat ice-cream (see
  recipe on page 110)

fresh pineapple, grapes, kiwi fruit
  and mango (for garnish)

Fold pineapple and passionfruit pulp through ice-cream
prior to freezing. Pour mixture into a mould and freeze.

To serve, quickly immerse mould in hot water for a few
seconds. Turn mould onto a serving plate and decorate
with pieces of fresh pineapple, grapes, kiwi fruit and slices
of fresh mango.

Pineapple tugboats Serves 4

2 large pineapples
3 oranges

3 ripe pears
pulp of 6 passionfruit

Cut pineapples in half lengthwise, including the green top. Carefully cut away pineapple flesh to create 4 pineapple shells. Chop up pineapple flesh.

Peel oranges and segment. Core pears, peel and cut into large chunks. Remove passionfruit pulp and add to remaining fruit. Toss lightly so all fruits are coated with passionfruit. Spoon fruit into pineapple boats and chill well before serving. Serve with low-fat ice-cream or low-fat yoghurt.

Platter of figs with date and walnut cream
Serves 6–8

8 ripe figs
1 cup low-fat yoghurt
2 teaspoons vanilla essence
6 fresh dates, stoned

2 tablespoons finely chopped walnuts
1 teaspoon finely grated lemon rind

Cut figs in half and arrange on a serving platter. Combine yoghurt, vanilla and dates, and purée. Fold in walnuts and lemon rind. Pour the date and walnut cream over the figs and serve.

Steamed
date pudding   Serves 4-6

1 cup chopped dates
1 cup sultanas
$^1/_2$ cup fresh orange juice
1 teaspoon mixed spice
grated rind of 1 lemon

1 cup unbleached wholemeal self-
  raising flour
1 teaspoon bicarb of soda
$^1/_2$ cup low-fat milk
1 dessertspoon vinegar

Place dates, sultanas, orange juice, mixed spice and lemon rind in a saucepan. Gently simmer for 3 minutes. Leave to cool slightly.

Sift flour and bicarb of soda. Add flour to fruit mixture. Combine milk and vinegar and stir into mixture. Line a small pudding basin with non-stick baking paper. Spoon in mixture. Cover with a sheet of non-stick baking paper and seal with pudding basin lid. Place in a saucepan of boiling water, cover, and keep boiling for 1 hour. Replace water if necessary.

Steamed fruit pudding Serves 4-6

½ cup currants
1 cup diced dried apricots
½ cup mixed peel
½ teaspoon ground cinnamon
⅛ teaspoon nutmeg
⅛ teaspoon ground cloves

½ cup fresh orange juice
1 cup unbleached wholemeal self-raising flour
¼ cup low-fat milk
1 egg white, beaten

Line a pudding basin with non-stick baking paper. Place fruits, spices and orange juice in a saucepan and simmer for 5 minutes. Allow to cool but not to get cold. Sift flour and return husks. Add flour to fruit mixture, then add milk and egg white and stir well. Pour into pudding basin, cover with a sheet of non-stick baking paper and seal with pudding basin lid.

Place in a large saucepan with boiling water. Steam pudding for 1–1½ hours. Do not let saucepan boil dry; water in saucepan should be boiling constantly. Serve with low-fat custard, low-fat yoghurt or low-fat ice-cream. Leftover pudding can be refrigerated, sliced thinly and served to accompany a cup of tea.

Strawberries
in brandy and orange syrup   Serves 4

2 punnets strawberries
1 cup fresh orange juice
1 tablespoon brandy
1 teaspoon finely grated orange
  rind

2 tablespoons apple juice
  concentrate

Hull strawberries and purée a quarter of the quantity with remaining ingredients. Pour syrup over remaining strawberries and chill well. Serve with low-fat ice-cream.

Strawberry
ice-cream cake   Serves 8-10

1 litre low-fat ice-cream (see
  recipe on page 110)
3 punnets strawberries, washed
  and hulled

$^1/_2$ cup toasted almond flakes (for
  garnish)
extra strawberries (for garnish)

Make ice-cream as per recipe, but do not freeze in the final step. Pour a third of the ice-cream into a foil-lined round tin. Slice strawberries finely and use half in a layer on top of the ice-cream mixture. Pour half of remaining ice-cream mixture over the top. Add another layer of strawberries, then pour the remaining ice-cream over the top and freeze.

To serve, turn out of tin, remove foil and place on a serving plate. Allow to soften slightly. Sprinkle with almond flakes and decorate the edge of the cake with fresh whole strawberries.

Winter
fruit salad Serves 4–6

$\frac{1}{2}$ cup halved and stoned fresh
dates
$\frac{1}{2}$ cup halved and stoned prunes
$\frac{1}{2}$ cup halved dried figs, stalks
removed

$\frac{1}{3}$ cup whole unblanched almonds
$\frac{1}{4}$ cup walnut halves
1 teaspoon cinnamon
1 cup fresh orange juice

Combine dried fruits and nuts and place in a clean jar.
Add cinnamon to orange juice and pour over the top.
Shake to coat the fruit with the liquid. Allow to soak for
at least 4 hours. Serve with low-fat ice-cream, low-fat
yoghurt or low-fat custard, with pancakes or over slices of
fresh cantaloupe, pawpaw or pineapple.

Note Store in the refrigerator. This fruit salad can be stored
for several weeks.

Yoghurt
cheese pie Serves 8–10

BASE
$\frac{1}{2}$ cup wheatgerm
$\frac{1}{3}$ cup almond meal

FILLING
1 cup low-fat yoghurt
250 g low-fat cream cheese or
  cottage cheese or tofu

2 tablespoons honey or apple
  juice concentrate
$\frac{1}{2}$ teaspoon vanilla essence
1 teaspoon grated orange rind
1 tablespoon gelatine
2 tablespoons hot water
sprinkle of nutmeg

To make the base, combine base ingredients and spread evenly over a lined 20-cm cake tin.

To make the filling, beat the first five filling ingredients until smooth and creamy. Sprinkle gelatine over hot water and stir until dissolved. Let cool slightly. Fold through yoghurt mixture and pour over base. Refrigerate until firm. Sprinkle lightly with nutmeg. Cut into slices and serve garnished with your choice of fresh seasonal fruit.

Cakes, breads and pastry

Apple slice

BASE
1 cup wheatgerm
$^1/_2$ cup shredded coconut
$^1/_2$ cup almond meal
60 g cottage cheese

FILLING
1 x 800 g can unsweetened cooked
  apples, well drained

2 teaspoons finely grated lemon
  rind
1 teaspoon cinnamon

TOPPING
1 cup flaked almonds

To make the base, place all base ingredients in a food processor and blend until well combined. Press mixture into a lined lamington tin.

To make the filling, combine all filling ingredients and spread evenly over base. Cover the top with almonds. Bake at 180°C for 30–40 minutes.

Note Other fruits may be substituted for apple.

Apricot loaf

1 cup bran
1 cup chopped dried apricots
$^3/_4$ cup mixed peel

2 cups low-fat milk
$1^1/_2$ cups unbleached wholemeal
  self-raising flour

Mix bran, apricots, mixed peel and milk in a bowl and let stand for 2 hours. Sift flour and return husks. Add small amounts of flour and stir well until all ingredients are thoroughly mixed. Spoon mixture into a lined non-stick loaf tin and bake at 180°C for 30–40 minutes or until firm.

Bran fruit loaf

1 cup bran
1 cup chopped apricots
$^3/_4$ cup raisins
1$^3/_4$ cups low-fat milk

1$^1/_2$ cups unbleached wholemeal
  self-raising flour
extra bran

Mix bran, apricots, raisins and milk in a bowl and let stand for 2 hours. Sift flour and return husks. Add small amounts of flour and stir well until all ingredients are thoroughly mixed. Sprinkle top of cake with extra bran. Spoon mixture into a lined non-stick loaf tin and bake at 180°C for 30–40 minutes or until firm.

Carrot loaf

2 cups unbleached wholemeal
  self-raising flour
1 teaspoon bicarb of soda
1 teaspoon nutmeg
1 cup chopped raisins

$^1/_2$ cup chopped walnuts
1$^1/_2$ cups grated carrot
2 egg whites
$^1/_2$ cup low-fat yoghurt
1 cup low-fat milk

Sift flour, bicarb of soda and nutmeg into a bowl. Return husks. Stir in raisins, walnuts and carrot. Beat egg whites, yoghurt and milk. Pour into other ingredients and beat well. Spoon mixture into a lined non-stick loaf tin and bake at 170°C for 40–60 minutes.

Easy wholemeal bread
Makes 3 loaves or 2 dozen rolls or 6 French sticks

60 g compressed yeast
800 ml warm water
400 ml warm low-fat milk
5 cups unbleached white plain
  flour

5 cups unbleached wholemeal
  plain flour

Combine yeast, water and milk. Stir to dissolve yeast.
Sift flours into a large bowl. Make a well in the centre and
pour in yeast mixture. Move flour from sides of the bowl
and sprinkle lightly over mixture. Leave in a warm place
for approximately 20 minutes to allow yeast to sponge.
Mix thoroughly with a long straight-edged knife or
spatula until all flour is absorbed. The mixture should be
quite tacky.

Flour bench very well and empty dough onto it. It will be
very sticky, so continue to use the knife or spatula and
turn over dough from the sides to the centre until dough
is completely covered in flour. Place in a clean, lightly
oiled bowl and set aside to rise. Leave for approximately
40 minutes to 1 hour.

When dough has risen approximately 5 cm, empty out
again onto a well-floured board or bench and lightly turn
over dough – outside edges to centre.

To form loaves, cut into 6 equal parts to make 3 high tin
loaves. Place 2 parts in each lightly oiled tin and set aside
for dough to double in size or to reach the top of the tin.
Brush top with water or low-fat milk. Sprinkle with
poppy seeds, caraway seeds, cracked wheat, rolled oats,
wheat flakes or fresh herbs. Bake at 180°C for 30–40
minutes.

To form rolls, take small pieces of dough, roll out like a
sausage and tie in a knot. Top as for loaves. Place rolls side

by side on a lightly oiled baking tray. Bake at 180°C for 25–30 minutes.

To form French sticks, divide dough into 6 equal parts. Roll out each part like a sausage. These sticks will rise nicely if cooked in a lightly oiled French stick tin. Top as for loaves. Make slits along the top of sticks with a knife. Bake at 180°C for 20–25 minutes.

VARIATIONS

Garlic bread
Add 1 tablespoon or more of garlic powder.

Grain bread
Add ½ cup mixed grain mixture (available at health food stores). Add more water if dough becomes too dry.

Herb bread
Add 2 tablespoons or more of your favourite fresh herb (parsley, chives, oregano, basil) finely chopped.

Oatmeal bread
Add 1 cup rolled oats. Add more water or low-fat milk if dough becomes too dry.

Onion bread
Add 1 tablespoon or more of onion powder or dried onion flakes.

Spiced fruit bread
Add 2 teaspoons mixed spice, 1 teaspoon cinnamon and 1 cup finely minced mixed dried fruit.

Sweet bread
Add 2 tablespoons or more finely chopped lemon rind, orange rind or mandarin rind.

Note Bread should be eaten immediately or stored in refrigerator. Recipe is suitable for freezing.

Filled apple cake

4 egg whites	1 teaspoon vanilla essence
125 g minced dried apple	1 cup unbleached wholemeal self-
¼ cup low-fat milk	raising flour
1 dessertspoon vinegar	2 teaspoons baking powder

Beat egg whites until stiff. Mince apple in a food processor. Combine milk and vinegar. Fold in apple, milk with vinegar, and vanilla. Sift dry ingredients and add to the egg white mixture. Fold through gently until all flour is combined. Line a 20-cm round springform cake tin with non-stick baking paper. Spoon mixture into cake tin. Bake at 170°C for 30–40 minutes. Turn out and cool.

FILLINGS
Apple filling
1 quantity apple spread (see
  recipe on page 154)

Cut cake into 3 layers and spread each layer with apple spread. Place cake in the refrigerator for 24 hours before cutting. Lightly dust with icing sugar before serving. Serve with low-fat custard.

Passionfruit filling

1 cup cottage cheese	2 tablespoons apple juice
pulp of 4 passionfruit	concentrate

Combine ingredients and beat well. Cut cake in half and spread filling over bottom layer. Place top layer on firmly and refrigerate cake until required. Lightly dust with icing sugar before serving.

Fruity pumpkin cake

125 g sultanas
125 g raisins
125 g mixed peel
125 g chopped dried apricots
1 tablespoon honey or apple juice concentrate
1 cup fresh orange juice or unsweetened apple juice

1 teaspoon bicarb of soda
1 cup cold cooked mashed pumpkin
1 teaspoon mixed spice
250 g unbleached wholemeal self-raising flour
4 egg whites

Combine first six ingredients in a saucepan. Bring to the boil, then turn down heat and simmer for 1 minute for fruits to soften. Remove from heat and add bicarb of soda. Allow to cool. Fold in pumpkin.

Sift spice and flour. Beat egg whites until stiff peaks form, and add to the flour. Stir the flour and egg white mixture into the fruit mixture in two lots. Spoon mixture into a 20-cm round non-stick cake tin lined with baking paper. Bake at 170°C for 1 hour or until cake is firm to touch, or when a wooden skewer inserted into the centre of the cake comes out dry and clean. Serve warm from the oven with low-fat custard or low-fat ice-cream.

Note This cake is best eaten within days of making. Keep refrigerated. Cake can be cut into portions, wrapped in plastic wrap and frozen.

Moist
mandarin and banana cake

3 very ripe bananas or 1 banana
  and 2 grated Granny Smith
  apples
1 cup stoned dates
peel from $^1/_2$ mandarin (remove
  pith)
125 g cottage cheese

4 egg whites
1 teaspoon vanilla essence
2 tablespoons chopped walnuts
$1^1/_2$ cups unbleached wholemeal
  self-raising flour
1 teaspoon bicarb of soda

Mash bananas. Place dates and mandarin peel in a food
processor and mince finely. Add cottage cheese and beat
until quite smooth. Add 1 egg white at a time. Add
bananas, vanilla and then walnuts. Sift flour and bicarb of
soda and fold through gently. Spoon into a lightly oiled
20-cm ring tin or a 20-cm deep fluted tin. Bake at 170°C
for 30–40 minutes or until cake is firm.

VARIATION

Substitute ¾ cup apricot pulp for bananas. Omit mandarin
peel. Spoon mixture into paper patty pans. Bake at 170°C
for 10–15 minutes. (Makes approximately 30 small cakes.)

Note This is a versatile cake recipe, so feel free to use any
fruit or fruit combination. The quantity of fruit should be
¾ cup. You could substitute orange or lemon peel for
mandarin peel.

Muesli loaf

2 cups unbleached wholemeal
   self-raising flour
1 teaspoon mixed spice
30 g low-fat yoghurt
1 cup low-fat toasted muesli

$1/2$ cup chopped raisins
1 cup grated raw carrot
1 egg white, lightly beaten
1 cup low-fat milk

Sift flour and spice into a bowl. Stir in yoghurt. Add toasted muesli, raisins and carrot, and mix well. Fold in egg white and milk until well combined. Turn into a 25 x 10-cm loaf tin lined with baking paper. Bake at 170°C for 40–60 minutes.

No-bake festive cake

375 g prunes
1 cup unsweetened apple juice
8 cups crushed Vita-Brits
125 g chopped dates
155 g chopped raisins
90 g walnuts
2 teaspoons finely grated orange
   rind

1 teaspoon finely grated lemon rind
$3/4$ cup sultanas or apricots or
   dried apple
$1/2$ teaspoon cinnamon
$1/2$ teaspoon ginger
$1/2$ cup fresh orange juice
2 teaspoons brandy or rum

Cook prunes in apple juice until tender. Drain well, and set juice aside. Chop prunes finely. Combine all ingredients, including juice, and mix well. Pack mixture into a 20-cm foil-lined cake tin. Press down firmly and cover with foil. Refrigerate for at least 3 hours before cutting.

Pikelets

Makes 12

1 cup unbleached wholemeal plain
  flour
2 tablespoons skim milk powder
3 teaspoons baking powder

1 cup low-fat milk or low-fat
  soymilk
2 whole eggs or 3 egg whites

Blend all ingredients. Leave to stand for 30 minutes before cooking. Drop spoonfuls of mixture onto a lightly oiled non-stick pan. Cook until mixture bubbles. Turn and cook to brown other side. Serve with low-fat cottage cheese, chopped dried fruit, sultanas, currants, chopped fresh fruit, or sugar-free jam spreads.

Raisin puffs

Makes 12

2 cups soy flour
4 teaspoons baking powder
1 cup chopped raisins
2 teaspoons finely grated orange
  or lemon rind

1 dessertspoon honey or apple
  juice concentrate
1–1$\frac{1}{2}$ cups low-fat milk
60 g finely minced dried apple

Sift flour and baking powder twice. Add raisins, orange or lemon rind, and honey or apple juice concentrate. Stir, adding milk. (Mixture should be slightly sticky.) Add apple. Spoon mixture into paper muffin cases. Bake at 170°C for 20 minutes or until tops are golden brown. Turn out onto a cooling rack to cool. Break open and fill with apple spread or apricot fruit spread.

Savoury bread loaf

1/2 cup buckwheat
8–10 slices wholemeal bread, crumbed
1 carrot, grated
1 small onion, finely chopped
2 small Granny Smith apples, peeled and grated

1 cup finely chopped celery
1/2 cup seeded and finely chopped red capsicum
2 tablespoons date and apple chutney (see recipe on page 155)
1 egg white
black pepper

Combine all ingredients and mix well. Press into a lightly oiled 25 x 10-cm loaf tin and place in a water bath. Bake at 180°C for 30 minutes. Remove from oven and let cool in tin. Turn out and refrigerate.

Note This loaf can be sliced and used as a meat substitute served with salad, or it can be sliced onto dry biscuits topped with tomato and alfalfa sprouts.

Sesame fruit loaf

1 cup All Bran
1 cup low-fat milk
1 cup wheatgerm
1 teaspoon bicarb of soda
1/2 cup sultanas
1/2 cup currants

1/2 cup raisins
1/2 cup chopped walnuts
1 tablespoon honey or apple juice concentrate
toasted sesame seeds

Soak bran in milk for 5 minutes. Add remaining ingredients – except sesame seeds – and mix thoroughly. Spoon into a 25 x 10-cm loaf tin lined with baking paper. Sprinkle with toasted sesame seeds. Bake at 170°C for 35–40 minutes.

Sesame
scone roll

2 cups unbleached wholemeal
  self-raising flour
$^1/_2$ cup low-fat yoghurt
1 dessertspoon fresh lemon juice
$^3/_4$ cup low-fat milk

FILLING
1 medium onion, grated
1 carrot, grated
1 green capsicum, seeded and
  finely diced

1 large potato, peeled and grated
1 tablespoon tabouleh (see recipe
  on page 55)
1 tablespoon finely chopped fresh
  parsley
1 tablespoon finely chopped fresh
  mint
$^1/_2$ teaspoon basil
extra low-fat yoghurt
$^1/_2$ cup sesame seeds

To make the scone, place flour and yoghurt in a food processor and blend until mixture resembles fine breadcrumbs. Combine lemon juice and milk. Make a well in the flour and yoghurt mixture and pour in lemon juice and milk. Knead mixture on a lightly floured board and roll out to a 2-cm thick square or rectangle.

To make the filling, combine all filling ingredients – except yoghurt and sesame seeds. Spread over scone mixture and roll up. Dampen top of scone roll with a little extra yoghurt and sprinkle with sesame seeds. Bake at 200°C for 10 minutes. Turn down to 180°C and bake for a further 10–15 minutes. Slice and serve.

VARIATION
Cook scone roll for 20 minutes then remove from oven. Cut into 5-cm slices. Form a circle with the slices on a serving platter. Sprinkle over finely grated low-fat grating cheese. Serve with salad in the centre.

Wheatgerm pastry

180 g unbleached wholemeal plain
  flour, sifted
60 g wheatgerm

90 g cottage cheese
1 tablespoon fresh lemon juice

Combine all ingredients (preferably in a food processor) until mixture becomes a smooth ball. Refrigerate for 1 hour before using. Knead lightly on a floured board and roll out to required size. If lining a pie dish, use a fork to make air holes in base and sides of pastry case.

Note This pastry recipe should not be likened to puff pastry or shortcrust pastry. It is both a casing for pies or pasties and a tasty way of adding roughage to your diet. It should be cooked at a low to moderate temperature until filling is cooked and pastry is just lightly browned. (If cooked in a very hot oven, the pastry becomes quite brittle.) The quantity is enough to line and top a 20-cm pie dish or line a large pie dish, and makes approximately 6 average-sized pasties.

Wholemeal
potato pastry

250 g unbleached plain flour,
  sifted
1 medium potato, peeled and
  finely grated

$1/3$ cup water
3 tablespoons fresh lemon juice

Combine all ingredients (preferably in a food processor) until mixture becomes a smooth ball. Refrigerate for 1 hour before using. Knead lightly on a floured board and roll out to required size. Leave pastry to rest while preparing filling.

Note This pastry recipe should not be likened to puff pastry or shortcrust pastry. It is both a casing for pies or pasties and a tasty way of adding roughage to your diet. It should be cooked at a low to moderate temperature until filling is cooked and pastry is just lightly browned. (If cooked in a very hot oven, the pastry becomes quite brittle.) The quantity is enough to line and top a 20-cm pie dish or line a large pie dish, and makes approximately 6 average-sized pasties.

Drinks

Apple milk drink Serves 2

1 cup fresh or unsweetened apple
  juice, well chilled
1 cup low-fat milk or low-fat
  soymilk, well chilled

sprinkle of cinnamon

Blend until thick and foamy. Sprinkle with cinnamon.

Apricot and vanilla drink Serves 1

1 cup low-fat milk or low-fat
  soymilk

4 fresh apricots, stoned
1 teaspoon vanilla essence

Blend until thick and foamy.

Banana milk Serves 1

1 cup low-fat milk or low-fat
  soymilk
1 banana, peeled and mashed

2 teaspoons skim milk powder
1 teaspoon brewer's yeast
sprinkle of nutmeg

Blend until thick and foamy. Sprinkle with nutmeg.

Note Brewer's yeast is high in vitamin B and is an
excellent food supplement to add to your diet.

Barley water <small>Serves 6–8</small>

3 tablespoons pearl barley
9 cups water
1 tablespoon honey or apple juice
  concentrate

fresh juice and peel of 2 oranges
fresh juice and peel of 2 lemons

Place barley in a small saucepan. Add enough water to cover. Bring to the boil. Remove from heat, strain and discard water. Cover barley with 9 cups of water, bring to the boil and simmer for 15 minutes.

Place honey or apple juice concentrate, and the juice and peel of oranges and lemons in a large jug. Pour barley water in through a sieve. Discard barley. Leave to cool. Remove peel and refrigerate.

Note This is an excellent thirst-quencher or a pick-me-up if you're not feeling well.

Fruit
and vegetable cocktails Serves 1

$1/2$–1 cup water, well chilled

COCKTAIL COMBINATIONS

◆ 1 apple, 1 carrot, 1 stick celery

◆ 4 carrots, ¼ lemon (peel included), sprigs of fresh parsley

◆ 1 apple, flesh of 1 orange, flesh of 1 mango

◆ 3 slices pineapple, 1 carrot, 1 small wedge of lemon (peel included)

◆ flesh of 1 grapefruit, flesh of 1 orange, 2 slices pineapple

◆ 2 apples, flesh of 2 kiwi fruit, ¼ cup chopped fresh mint

◆ flesh of 1 orange, 1 cup hulled strawberries, ¼ lemon, ¼ cup chopped fresh mint

Add water and one of the cocktail combinations and place in a blender. Process, strain and pour juice into a glass. Garnish with iceblocks, a slice of lemon or orange, mint, parsley, cucumber peel, cherries or strawberries. Try topping up with soda water for a variation.

Fruit cup   Serves 6

2 cups fresh orange juice
2 cups fresh or unsweetened
    apple juice
2 cups fresh or unsweetened
    pineapple juice

$1/2$ cup passionfruit pulp
iceblocks
soda water or mineral water

Combine juices. Stir through ½ cup passionfruit pulp. Add iceblocks and dilute with mineral water or soda water.

Island thirst quencher   Serves 1

125 ml fresh or unsweetened
    pineapple juice
$1/4$ cup unsweetened pineapple
    pieces, drained

soda water
chopped fresh mint (for garnish)
125 ml low-fat yoghurt

Blend all ingredients and top up with soda water to your desired taste. Garnish with chopped mint.

Orange milk   Serves 1

1 cup fresh orange juice
2 teaspoons skim milk powder
$1/4$ teaspoon vanilla essence

$1/4$ cup low-fat ice-cream (see
    recipe on page 110)

Blend until thick and frothy.

Pineapple milk shake Serves 1

1 cup low-fat milk, well chilled
2 teaspoons skim milk powder or
  1 tablespoon low-fat ice-cream
  (see recipe on page 110)

³/₄ cup fresh or unsweetened
  pineapple juice, well chilled
fresh mint (for garnish)

Blend until thick and foamy. Garnish with mint.

Summer party punch Serves 10–14

1 litre fresh orange juice
500 ml fresh or unsweetened
  pineapple juice
500 g strawberries, hulled and
  puréed
1¹/₂ litres soda water
iceblocks

FRUIT KEBABS (for garnish)
peeled Granny Smith apple cubes
pineapple chunks
strawberries

Combine orange juice, pineapple juice and strawberries and chill well. Add soda water and iceblocks prior to serving. Garnish each glass with a fruit kebab.

To make the fruit kebabs, thread fruit through cocktail sticks and place one in each glass.

Dressings

Creamy
tangy yoghurt dressing Makes 1 cup

½ cup low-fat yoghurt
¼ teaspoon dill
1 tablespoon fresh lemon juice

½ cup coarsely grated peeled
  cucumber
ground black pepper

Combine all ingredients and chill.

Note This could also be used as a dip to serve with a platter of raw vegetables.

French
dressing Makes 1 cup

2 tablespoons finely chopped
  fresh basil or 1 teaspoon basil
½ teaspoon black pepper
½ cup fresh lemon juice
2 tablespoons finely chopped
  fresh parsley

2 teaspoons finely grated lemon
  rind
⅔ cup white-wine vinegar
1 tablespoon apple juice
  concentrate

Place all ingredients in a sealed jar. Shake well and store in the refrigerator.

Fruity dressing   Makes 2 cups

1 cup fresh orange juice
$^1/_2$ cup fresh lemon juice
2 tablespoons apple juice
  concentrate
$^1/_2$ cucumber, peeled and seeded
2 cloves garlic, crushed
1 tablespoon finely grated lemon
  rind

1 tablespoon finely grated orange
  rind
2 tablespoons chopped fresh
  herbs (parsley, basil, chives,
  thyme)

Combine all ingredients – except lemon and orange rind
and fresh herbs – and blend in a food processor. Add other
ingredients but do not blend. Shake well and store in
sealed jars in the refrigerator.

Homestyle ricotta cheese   Makes approximately 2 cups

$4^1/_2$ litres low-fat milk

$^1/_3$ cup fresh lemon juice

Scald milk then remove from heat. Add lemon juice. Let
stand for at least 20 minutes. Pour into a basin lined with
cheesecloth. Lift cheesecloth edges to strain liquid (whey)
from the curds, pressing the curds to remove as much
liquid as possible. Chill the mass of ricotta cheese that
remains. Use as required.

Homestyle
yoghurt
Makes 3–4 cups

1 litre low-fat milk

4 tablespoons skim milk powder

2 tablespoons commercial yoghurt

Pour milk into a saucepan. Add milk powder and stir until dissolved. Heat milk gently until it reaches boiling point. Cool until tepid.

Blend a little milk with yoghurt until smooth, then stir back into remaining milk. Pour mixture into a sterilised wide-mouthed vacuum flask. Cover and stand for 4–6 hours, by which time it should set to a firm yoghurt. Do not disturb until yoghurt has set. Refrigerate.

VARIATION

1½ cups skim milk powder

600 ml hot water

3 tablespoons commercial yoghurt

Place skim milk powder in basin and make a well in the centre. Gradually stir in water and whisk until milk powder has dissolved. Blend ½ cup of this milk with yoghurt until smooth, then stir back into remaining milk. Pour mixture into a sterilised wide-mouthed vacuum flask. Cover and stand for 4–6 hours, by which time it should set to a firm yoghurt. Do not disturb until yoghurt has set. Refrigerate.

Note It is best to start yoghurt-making using only fresh commercial yoghurt. Adding the yoghurt to milk hotter than 45°C will destroy the bacterial culture and prevent the setting action. Add any flavourings to yoghurt once it has set and before refrigerating.

Island dressing
Makes 1½ cups

½ cup low-fat yoghurt
½ cup ricotta cheese or mashed
  tofu
juice of 1 lemon
⅓ cup salt-free tomato paste
3 drops Tabasco

1 tablespoon seeded and chopped
  green capsicum
1 tablespoon finely chopped fresh
  parsley
1 tablespoon finely chopped fresh
  chives

Process all ingredients – except parsley and chives – until smooth. Add parsley and chives. Store in the refrigerator.

Low-fat sour cream
Makes 1 cup

½ cup low-fat yoghurt
½ cup ricotta cheese

squeeze of fresh lemon
black pepper

Purée all ingredients until smooth. Store in the refrigerator.

Mixed herb dressing
Makes 2½ cups

1 cup herb vinegar (see recipe on
  page 144)
1 cup unsweetened apple juice
juice of 1 lemon

½ cucumber, peeled and seeded
2 tablespoons finely chopped
  mixed fresh herbs (parsley,
  chives, thyme, dill)

Process first four ingredients. Add herbs. Place in sealed jar and store in the refrigerator.

Tangy yoghurt dressing

1 cup low-fat yoghurt
½ cucumber, peeled and coarsely
  grated
2 tablespoons chopped fresh
  parsley

2 tablespoons chopped fresh
  chives
1 tablespoon fresh lemon juice
1 tablespoon white-wine vinegar

Combine all ingredients and chill.

Tarragon vinegar

1 cup tarragon leaves picked just
  before flowering and washed
  well

5 cups white-wine vinegar
sprigs of fresh tarragon

Place tarragon leaves in a jar and pour vinegar over them.
Cover and let stand for 2–3 weeks. Shake frequently. Strain
and pour into sterilised jars. Place a sprig of tarragon in
each jar and seal. Use as required to flavour salad greens or
chargrilled vegetables.

VARIATIONS

Herb vinegar
Substitute tarragon leaves with 1 tablespoon each of
chopped fresh chives, marjoram, basil and parsley.

Lemon or orange vinegar
Substitute tarragon leaves with thinly peeled rind of
2 oranges or 2 lemons.

Sauces

Cold date sauce Makes 2 cups

500 g finely chopped dates
1 cup fresh orange juice
1 tablespoon finely grated orange
  rind

1 cup low-fat yoghurt

Bring dates to the boil in orange juice and rind, and let simmer for 10 minutes or until dates are tender. Purée with yoghurt. Refrigerate. Serve date sauce with a platter of vegetables or fruit crudités, or serve with pancakes.

Gravy

Makes ¾ cup

2 tablespoons wholemeal plain
  flour
½ cup chicken stock (see recipe
  on page 40) or beef stock

½ cup commercial vegetable juice
½ cup water or dry white wine
black pepper

Brown flour in a saucepan or pan over low heat. Remove from heat and cool slightly. Add stock and beat to a smooth paste. Slowly add vegetable juice, water or wine, stirring constantly. Add pepper to taste. Let simmer gently for 2 minutes to thicken. (Alternatively, you can brown flour and then blend remaining ingredients. Return to saucepan and cook for 5 minutes or until gravy has thickened.)

Herb sauce Makes 1 cup

1 cup low-fat yoghurt
1 teaspoon Dijon mustard
1$\frac{1}{2}$ tablespoons white-wine
  vinegar
$\frac{1}{2}$ tablespoon fresh lemon juice

black pepper
1 tablespoon chopped fresh chives
1 tablespoon chopped fresh dill
1 tablespoon chopped fresh
  parsley

Purée yoghurt, mustard, vinegar, lemon juice and pepper.
Add chives, dill and parsley. Refrigerate.

Horseradish cream Makes $\frac{1}{2}$ cup

$\frac{1}{2}$ cup cottage cheese or tofu
1 tablespoon grated horseradish

1 tablespoon finely chopped
  chives

Combine all ingredients.

Low-fat custard

INGREDIENT	MAKES 2 CUPS	MAKES 3 CUPS	MAKES 1 LITRE	MAKES 2 LITRES
MILK	2 cups	3 cups	1 litre	2 litres
CORNFLOUR	$^1/_2$ cup	$^3/_4$ cup	1 cup	2 cups
VANILLA ESSENCE	1 tspn	$1^1/_2$ tspn	2 tspn	1 tbsp
ORANGE ZEST	2 tspn	1 tbsp	1 tbsp	2 tbsp
APPLE JUICE CONCENTRATE	$^1/_4$ cup	$^1/_3$ cup	$^1/_2$ cup	1 cup
LOW-FAT YOGHURT	$^1/_2$ cup	$^3/_4$ cup	1 cup	2 cups

Mix a little milk with cornflour to make a paste. Add cornflour mixture to remaining milk, vanilla essence and orange zest in a saucepan. Slowly bring to the boil, stirring continuously until custard begins to thicken.

Remove custard from the heat and stir in apple juice concentrate and yoghurt.

Note This recipe is ideal for desserts that require a custard to set firm. It can be made with low-fat milk or soymilk. The orange zest colours the custard as well as adding flavour. The yoghurt adds a creamy texture.

Low-fat
mayonnaise Makes 1 cup

1 cup low-fat yoghurt
2 teaspoons fresh lemon juice
1 teaspoon dry mustard

$^1/_2$ teaspoon paprika
black pepper

Place all ingredients into a jar and shake. Refrigerate.

Mushroom
sauce Makes 2 cups

1 kg peeled and sliced mushrooms
$^1/_4$ cup water
2 tablespoons cornflour

pinch salt
black pepper

Place mushrooms in a saucepan with water. Let simmer
very gently with lid on for 30 minutes. (The mushrooms
will make their own juice.) Combine a little extra water
and cornflour to make a paste. Stir this into mushrooms
and cook for a further 2 minutes. Add a pinch of salt and
pepper to taste. Serve on hot wholemeal toast, over
cooked vegetables or as a pasta sauce.

Mustard
and dill sauce Makes $^1/_2$ cup

$^1/_4$ cup low-fat yoghurt
$1^1/_2$ tablespoons Dijon mustard

juice of $^1/_2$ lemon
2 tablespoons chopped fresh dill

Slowly add yoghurt to mustard, mixing continuously until
all yoghurt has been added. Stir in lemon juice and dill.

Plum sauce Makes 2 cups

1 kg stoned plums
2 onions, diced
bouquet garni (see page 19)
1 cup fresh orange juice

1 cup water
2 teaspoons grated fresh ginger
$^1/_4$ teaspoon cloves
$^1/_4$ teaspoon peppercorns

Place all ingredients in a saucepan. Cook over low heat, stirring regularly, for 1 hour or until mixture has reduced and thickened. Pour into sterilised jars and seal. Allow to cool and refrigerate. Serve with cold meats, add to stirfries or use as a dipping sauce.

Sweet and sour sauce Makes 2$^1/_2$ cups

1 x 500 ml can commercial
   vegetable juice
1 teaspoon cornflour
$^1/_2$ cup unsweetened pineapple
   juice
$^1/_2$ cup unsweetened pineapple
   pieces
2 tablespoons white-wine vinegar

black pepper
2 tablespoons tomato paste
$^1/_2$ cup seeded and chopped red
   and green capsicum
$^1/_2$ tablespoon finely chopped
   fresh parsley
$^1/_2$ tablespoon finely chopped
   fresh chives

Mix a little vegetable juice with cornflour to make a paste. Combine with remaining ingredients – except parsley and chives – in a small saucepan. Bring to the boil and simmer until sauce thickens and capsicum are cooked. Add parsley and chives.

Tomato capsicum sauce Makes 2½ cups

1 green capsicum, seeded and
  sliced into rings
½ cup finely sliced celery
½ medium onion, finely chopped
1½ cups water or chicken stock
  (see recipe on page 40)

1 x 425 g can salt-free tomatoes
  and juice
2 tablespoons salt-free tomato
  paste
3 drops Tabasco
2 spring onions, finely chopped

Cook capsicum, celery and onion in water or chicken
stock until soft. Add remaining ingredients and simmer for
10 minutes. Liquid should reduce to create a sauce thick
enough for serving.

Tomato relish Makes 1 litre

1.5 kg peeled, seeded and cubed
  ripe tomatoes
500 g diced mild onions
2 cups fresh orange juice
3 teaspoons curry powder

¼ teaspoon chilli powder
1 tablespoon dry mustard
2 cups white-wine or cider vinegar
1 cup raisins or sultanas (optional)

Place all ingredients in a large saucepan. Slowly bring to
the boil over a low heat and boil for 5 minutes. Reduce
heat and simmer for an hour or until mixture has
thickened. Pour into sterilised jars, cool and seal.
Refrigerate.

Note This sauce is excellent with cold meats and
vegetables, and as a sandwich spread, a spicy pizza sauce, a
filling for jacket potatoes and jaffles, and a dipping sauce.

Tomato
sauce Makes 1 litre

2 cloves garlic, crushed
1 onion, finely diced
1 kg tomatoes peeled, seeded and
  chopped
2 cups fresh orange juice
1 cup grated carrot
pinch mace
$^1/_2$ teaspoon dried oregano
1 tablespoon finely chopped fresh
  basil or 1 teaspoon basil

1 tablespoon finely chopped fresh
  parsley
2 teaspoons finely grated orange
  rind
1 cup dry white wine or chicken
  stock (see recipe on page 40)
black pepper
pinch salt

Place all ingredients – except pepper and salt – in a large
saucepan. Slowly bring to the boil over a low heat. Boil
for 5 minutes. Reduce heat and simmer until sauce
thickens. Add pepper and salt to taste. Pour into sterilised
jars, cool and seal. Refrigerate.

White
sauce Makes 1 cup

1 cup low-fat milk
2 tablespoons cornflour

black pepper

Pour ¾ cup of milk into a saucepan and heat to near
boiling. Mix cornflour with remaining milk to make a
paste. Add to hot milk, stirring continuously until sauce
boils and thickens. Add pepper to taste. Serve immediately.

Note Variations to this recipe include 2 tablespoons
grated low-fat grating cheese or chopped fresh chives; and
2 teaspoons Dijon mustard or chopped fresh mint or dill.

Spreads

Apple spread
<small>Makes 2 cups</small>

220 g dried apples
3 cups unsweetened pineapple
  juice
$\frac{1}{2}$ lemon

2 teaspoons finely grated lemon
  rind
2 teaspoons cinnamon

Combine all ingredients in a large saucepan. Simmer until apples are soft. Remove lemon. Purée and pour into sterilised jars. When cool, seal and store in the refrigerator. Serve on toast, scones, pikelets, pancakes or with low-fat ice-cream.

Apricot fruit spread
<small>Makes 2 cups</small>

125 g dried apricots
90 g dried apples
1 tablespoon finely grated orange
  rind

60 g raisins
$3\frac{1}{2}$ cups fresh orange juice

Combine all ingredients in a large saucepan. Simmer until fruit is soft. Purée and pour into sterilised jars. When cool, seal and store in the refrigerator. Serve on toast, scones, pikelets, pancakes or with low-fat ice-cream.

Chicken spread Makes 2 cups

1 cup cold minced cooked chicken
  (no skin)
1 tablespoon grated mild onion
1 tablespoon finely chopped fresh
  parsley

1 cup minced blanched almonds
3 tablespoons low-fat mayonnaise
  (see recipe on page 149)
$1/4$ teaspoon thyme
1 teaspoon fresh lemon juice

Blend all ingredients until smooth. Pour into a small bowl
and refrigerate. Serve with wholemeal toast fingers or
fresh wholemeal bread and salad greens.

Date and apple chutney Makes 4 cups

4 medium Granny Smith apples,
  peeled and grated
500 g stoned, seeded and
  chopped dates
2 onions, finely chopped
1 cup raisins, sultanas or apricots

1 teaspoon chilli powder
2 cups fresh orange juice
6 whole cloves
$1/4$ teaspoon ground allspice
$1^1/2$ cups wine or cider vinegar

Place all ingredients in a large saucepan and bring to the
boil. Simmer, stirring occasionally for 1 hour or until
mixture has a thick, soft consistency. Spoon into sterilised
hot jars and seal when cooled. Store in the refrigerator.

Note This is an excellent spread for sandwiches, a dip for
vegetable and fruit platters, or a chutney with chicken
and fish.

Pear and orange spread
Makes 2 cups

500 g chopped dried pears
1 cup fresh orange juice
1 cup water

¹/₄ teaspoon nutmeg
¹/₄ teaspoon mixed spice
grated rind of 1 orange

Place pears in a saucepan. Add remaining ingredients. Slowly bring to the boil and gently simmer until pears are soft and at least half the liquid has been reduced. Remove from heat and purée. Pour into sterilised jars and seal when cooled. Store in the refrigerator. Serve on toast, scones, pikelets, pancakes or with low-fat ice-cream.

Plum spread
Makes 3 cups

1 kg stoned plums
4 cups fresh orange juice
2 teaspoons fresh lemon juice

finely grated rind of 1 orange
¹/₄ cup apple juice concentrate

Place all ingredients in a saucepan and simmer until liquid has reduced and plums are quite mushy. Pour into sterilised jars and seal when cooled. Serve on toast, scones, pikelets, pancakes or with low-fat ice-cream.

Salmon
and cucumber spread Makes 1 cup

1 x 210 g can salmon in water,
  drained
$^1/_2$ cucumber, peeled and seeded
$^1/_2$ small red capsicum, seeded and
  chopped

1 teaspoon fresh lemon juice
$^1/_2$ teaspoon paprika
2 tablespoons finely chopped
  fresh parsley

Blend all ingredients – except parsley – until smooth. Add
parsley. Pour into a small pot and refrigerate. Serve with
wholemeal toast triangles or wholewheat biscuits.

Savoury
spread Makes 2 cups

250 g ripe tomatoes, peeled,
  seeded and chopped
1 tablespoon grated onion
1 tablespoon grated low-fat
  grating cheese

1 tablespoon low-fat yoghurt
1 teaspoon mixed herbs
black pepper
$^1/_8$ teaspoon cayenne pepper
1–2 cups wholemeal breadcrumbs

Place all ingredients – except breadcrumbs – in a
saucepan. Slowly bring to the boil, turn down heat and
simmer for 5 minutes. Remove from heat. Add enough
wholemeal breadcrumbs to make a paste. Store in
the refrigerator.

Steak paste
Makes 2 cups

500 g lean topside steak
1 bay leaf
1 tablespoon water
$1/2$ teaspoon black pepper

$1/4$ teaspoon ground mace
$1/4$ teaspoon nutmeg
$1/4$ teaspoon cayenne pepper
squeeze of fresh lemon

Chop steak into small pieces. Remove all fat. Put all ingredients into a heatproof dish. Cover and steam gently for 3 hours. When cool, blend until smooth. Add lemon juice. Spoon into a serving bowl, cover, and refrigerate.

Note This paste is an excellent sandwich filler.

Strawberry spread
Makes 2 cups

4 Granny Smith apples, cored,
  peeled and sliced
250 g strawberries, washed and
  hulled
2 cups fresh orange juice

$1/2$–1 teaspoon cinnamon
grated rind of 1 orange
2 teaspoons fresh lemon juice
$1/4$ cup apple juice concentrate

Combine all ingredients in a saucepan. Slowly bring to the boil, turn down heat and simmer for approximately 40 minutes or until mixture thickens. Pour into sterilised jars and seal when cooled. Once seal is opened, jam should be kept refrigerated.

Stuffings

Apricot
and walnut stuffing   Makes 1½ cups

60 g chopped dried apricots
3–4 sticks celery, finely chopped
125 g finely chopped walnuts
1¼ cups wholemeal breadcrumbs
1 tablespoon chopped fresh
  parsley

2 spring onions (white part only),
  finely sliced
1 egg white

Combine all ingredients. Refrigerate until required.

Note This stuffing is excellent with chicken, turkey or fish.
Cut a pocket into the meat or roll the flattened meat or
fish around the filling and secure with toothpicks.

Fennel
stuffing   Makes 1 cup

1 small white onion, diced
1 cup soft wholemeal breadcrumbs
black pepper

2 tablespoons chopped fresh
  fennel leaves
2 tablespoons low-fat yoghurt

Combine all ingredients.

Note This stuffing is excellent with fish.

Parsley stuffing Makes 3 cups

3 cups wholemeal breadcrumbs
185 g chopped spring onions
1/2 cup chopped fresh parsley

black pepper
1 egg white

Combine all ingredients.

Potato and parsley stuffing Makes 1 1/2 cups

250 g cooked mashed potato
125 g buckwheat
60 g toasted unsalted cashews,
  almonds or macadamia nuts

1 medium white onion, diced
black pepper
1/2 cup chopped fresh parsley

Combine all ingredients.

Rice stuffing with herbs Makes 1 1/2 cups

1 cup cooked brown rice
1 medium white onion, diced
black pepper
3 tablespoons low-fat yoghurt

1/4 cup chopped fresh herbs of
  your choice (parsley, basil,
  coriander, oregano, chives,
  chervil, tarragon, dill, mint)

Combine all ingredients.

Note This is a great stuffing for red or green capsicum, tomatoes, zucchini, squash or cabbage leaves, or eggplant.

Sage and onion stuffing

Makes 1 cup

1 medium white onion, diced
125 g soft wholemeal breadcrumbs
black pepper
3 tablespoons chopped fresh sage
  or 2 teaspoons sage

1 egg white
¼ cup low-fat milk or
  3 tablespoons low-fat yoghurt

Combine all ingredients.

Index